Interest and Discipline
in Education

Students Library of Education

Interest and Discipline in Education

P. S. Wilson

Senior Lecturer in Education
Goldsmiths' College, University of London

London
Routledge & Kegan Paul

First published 1971
by Routledge and Kegan Paul Ltd
Broadway House,
68-74 Carter Lane,
London EC4V 5EL
Printed in Great Britain by
Northumberland Press Limited
Gateshead
© P. S. Wilson 1971
ISBN 0 7100 7049 7
Set in Linotype 10/12 Pilgrim

153.843

B/9253

THE STUDENTS LIBRARY OF EDUCATION has been designed to meet the needs of Students of Education at Colleges of Education and at University Institutes and Departments. It will also be valuable for practising teachers and educationists. The series takes full account of the latest developments in teacher-training and of new methods and approaches in education. Separate volumes will provide authoritative and up-to-date accounts of the topics within the major fields of sociology, philosophy and history of education, educational psychology and method. Care has been taken that specialist topics are treated lucidly and usefully for the non-specialist reader. Altogether, the Students Library of Education will provide a comprehensive introduction and guide to anyone concerned with the study of education and with educational theory and practice.

J. W. Tibble

The claim that education should be based on the 'needs and interests' of children has become more or less a slogan of the child-centred movement. It is often expressed in an extravagant and unguarded manner which obscures the important insights which it contains. Dr Wilson accepts such strictures, but he believes, nevertheless, that the notion of 'interest' is crucial to the elucidation of what education is as distinct from manipulating children, goading them, or just looking after them. With patience and thoroughness he attempts to disentangle what the connection is between 'interest' and 'education' and then proceeds to explore the relationship of 'interest' to 'discipline'.

Dr Wilson tackles many issues previously explored by John Dewey and his final position is somewhat similar. But he approaches these issues with more care and precision than Dewey ever displayed. Dr Wilson is a senior lecturer in education at Goldsmiths' College, University of London. His training in philosophy and his familiarity with conditions in modern and junior schools fit him very well for this task. His monograph fills an important gap in modern philosophy of education; for it is one of the first attempts at a precise and well-argued defence of a point of view associated with 'progressive' education.

Richard S. Peters

Contents

CONTENTS

viii

Introduction

By law, children have to go to school. Why should this be so?

At first sight one could find an easy sort of answer, I suppose, in terms of convenience. No doubt we have all wondered from time to time whether the daily practices of adults would be possible at all, if their children did not have to spend the greater part of the day at school. The trivially yet effectively disruptive character of children's activities is plain enough, from the adult point of view. The very fact that children's most serious occupations are lumped together by adults as 'play', points in the same direction. Towards the end of the school holidays, then, or during a teachers' strike, one might be tempted to say that children have to go to school so that adults can get on with their work.

But this would hardly seem to be a convincing answer, or at any rate hardly a *morally* convincing answer. In a moral community, there would have to be some more compelling reason than mere convenience, one would think, to justify sending children off to school under the law's compulsion.

Moreover, such an answer, in terms of the expediency of their being at school, would be even less satisfactory as an explanation not just of children's having to go to school, but also of their having to do certain sorts of things, rather than others, when they get there. Of course, in some schools it might actually be true that there are no particular reasons for what the children are doing there. Buildings can be so cramped, equipment so lacking, the administration so bizarre, and new teachers can come and go with such rapidity, that one may easily get the feeling that the real *point* of such institutions is simply to provide alternative daily accommodation to the streets, parks and houses from which the children have come. Indeed, I remember being told by a primary school headmaster on one occasion that he could see no reason for children being at his school, other than that it was warmer, drier and safer for them there than on the busy streets outside his gates. In the conditions under which he was working, he pointed out, this was the most that he could realistically hope to provide. Maybe there are more of such schools in existence than we think; but, however many or few of them there are, their existence does not seem to furnish a *morally* adequate reason for requiring children to receive schooling, and nor does it explain why in fact most schools still try, or claim, to provide something more for children than warmth, shelter, food and comparative safety from the world outside.

Before we can begin to look for further and perhaps better answers to the question with which I began, we must get clearer about the question itself, however, for it is really two in one. One question is, Why *should* children go to school? The other is, Why should they *have* to go? One question, in other words, is about the special character or features which for the most part we see and try to set up in the places which we call 'school', and in virtue of which we would try to justify our saying that children *should* go there. The other is a question about how we are to justify the *compulsion* which we are prepared to apply in order to get the children there, and to keep them there.

In the first two chapters of this book I shall be concerned with the first question, namely, the description and justification of what we mean by 'schooling'. Answers seem to fall broadly into two categories, each of which characterizes the special features of schooling in a different way. One sort of answer, seeing schooling as a means to the achievement of certain valuable goals lying beyond or outside the process itself, justifies it by pointing to its necessity as a prerequisite for reaching those ends. Children should go to school, in other words, because there are certain good things for which schooling is needed. In the chapter called 'Needs', therefore, I consider various examples of the sorts of good things or valuable goals which schooling is said to be needed for and thus justified by. One such 'needs-based' view of schooling I have already referred to above, in describing the belief that school is needed to protect the world of adults from the intrusive activities of children, or, to put it another way, that it is needed to protect children from the dangerous activities of adults. This, in a particular version, is the *sort* of view which the first chapter explores.

By contrast, in the second broad category of justifications and accounts of schooling, attempts are made to explain ways in which it may be valuable and justifiable in itself. On this view, the question 'Why should children go to school?' is answered by trying to explain what it means to say that there are or may be certain things about school which have a positive value of their own, rather than by pointing to various valuable goals or ends to which schooling is no more than a means. The discussion of one form of this view is undertaken in the chapter called 'Interests'.

In the chapters on 'Discipline' and 'Punishment', I turn to the question of compulsion. Even if we can satisfy ourselves as to why children *should* go to school, why should they *have* to? The same two questions could be asked, of course, about *any* compulsory social practice or about the compulsory membership of *any* social institution. For example, one could ask about the reasons for compulsory taxation, or for the compulsory registration of motor vehicles, or of infants' names. First, one would want to know why we *should* be taxed, or why we *should* keep a public record of the ownership of property such as motor-cars, or of the proper names of individuals. Second, though, even if it could be shown that such practices were valuable and worth engaging in on general grounds, the further question would still remain as to why people should *have* to engage in these practices, or in other words as to how we could justify *compelling* people to perform right actions and pursue good ends.

It is important to remember that the compulsion in these cases is deliberate. We are not talking here about respects in which these social practices might have to be engaged in in any case, regardless of the sanctions of the law. In a general sort of way one could argue, perhaps, that practices such as the communal pooling of individual resources, the public registration of property and the 'proper' naming of individuals are in any community *bound* to occur, in some way and to some extent. Without such practices, communities, in any sense of which we could conceive, could scarcely exist. But this would be a quite different kind of inevitability or 'compulsion', however, from the deliberate compulsion of the law. The particular *form* of pooling of resources represented by a system of taxation, and the particular *forms* of property registration and naming required by the Land Registry and the Registrar of Births, are socially contrived and avoidable, unlike the 'compulsions' of logic or of nature.

Similarly, although perhaps it is unavoidable that any member of a social group will be 'schooled' to some extent in the ways of that group, or in other words will be brought inevitably into some sort of conformity with its norms and practices, there is nothing inevitable or unavoidable about the particular *kind* of schooling which we have in mind when we say that children *have* to be sent to 'school'. Since there are no inescapable circumstances either of fact or of logic which could provide sufficient reasons for children's having to go to 'school' in this very particular sense, we must therefore ask what *moral* reasons there may be for the practice—unless, of course, we are prepared either to abandon compulsory schooling altogether, or to live in a non-moral community.

Such, then, is the general outline of this book. In the first two chapters, two different sorts of answer are considered to the question 'Why should children go to school?' The second two chapters consider aspects of the question 'Why should they *have* to go?' Throughout the book, however, the kind of schooling and the kind of compulsion with which I personally am most concerned is the kind which I believe one could most properly call 'educative'. It is therefore not just questions about compulsory schooling, and the morality of it, in which I am interested to find answers, but also questions about what we mean by saying that our schools, in total, constitute a system of 'education'.

Schooling and education are far from being coextensive things. 'Education', by comparison with 'schooling', is a term which seems to me, as it has seemed to others (e.g. Taylor, 1969), to need to be much more narrowly defined. Although most of what takes place in schools could be called 'schooling', only some of it (and not necessarily any of it) is 'educative'.

The distinction is a fairly familiar one. Roger Wilson, for example, once commented as follows upon Mark Twain's account of it:

> 'Take care that your son's schooling doesn't interfere with his education,' said Mark Twain to a friend. Contemporary society provides more and more schooling. Whose business is it to see that it is educational? (1965, p. 83)

My belief is that it is mainly the business of teachers, and it is to teachers and student-teachers, therefore, that this book is addressed.

Having said this, however, I must add at once that this is not a book about educational methods. It contains no prescriptions for any more or less efficient procedures or devices for getting things done in school, such as methods of 'getting children interested' or of 'disciplining' them. Rather, it is concerned with the prior question of what it is that one is planning to employ such 'methods' *to do*. Recently, for example, a teacher, knowing that I was interested in questions about punishment and assuming that this meant no more than that I had an interest in punitive *methods*, told me with the air of one imparting a valuable secret that he had found an infallible way of causing physical pain to children '... without even touching them!' This turned out to consist of creeping up silently behind them, and then, suddenly, clapping his hands together sharply, next to their ears. The moral of the story in the present context lies in that teacher's misinterpretation of the interest which I had shown in punishment. So far as I was concerned, I could think of only *one* 'way' or 'method' of punishing children (or of rewarding them, for that matter), namely, fairly. My interest in punishment, mistaken for an interest in methods of intentionally causing pain to wrongdoers, in fact was derived from an interest in what the term 'fairly' could possibly mean in various contexts, such as educational, economic, legal, sporting, and so on. By trying to work out what 'fairly' could mean, I hoped to get clearer about how to distinguish 'good' punishments from 'bad' ones.

Similarly, in what follows, by trying to investigate what notions such as 'interest' and 'discipline' could possibly mean in various contexts, I hope to get clearer about how to distinguish good from bad or indifferent schooling and education. Otherwise, to the extent that I remain vague as to what it is that the 'methods' are supposed to accomplish, *any* methods, old or new, will do.

Fashions in 'methods' sweep up and down the educational scene like tidal bores. Some teachers, retreating to a dry spot, sit sensibly still, knowing that in due course what comes in will go out, and vice versa. Others, maybe, allow themselves to be swept from place to place in an exciting, but ultimately exhausting, way. Neither of these strategies, I believe, helps children to make much sense of their schooling, or of education. No addition or subtraction merely of *methods* can make or unmake the *sense* of something. Unless, at the same time as trying out newer methods, we are trying also to think explicitly and carefully what 'education' means and what schooling is for, all methods equally, so far as we could see, would suffice for the job.

I

Needs

1 The notion of 'need'

Needs are prerequisites. To play patience, I need at least a pack of cards. To travel by train to Manchester, a Londoner needs the service from Euston. A batsman on 99 needs one more run for his century. A squeaky door probably needs oiling. In each of these different examples, what is prerequisite can never be identified in advance of making value judgments about desirable goals or ends. To discover what is needed in any situation, then, or to decide whether X is needed rather than Y, more is required than simple inspection of the facts of the case.

Knowing the facts is important, of course. For example, you may say that the flowers wilting in the hot sun on the lawn need watering. I may reply that what they need is a dose of weed-killer, since 'in fact' they happen to be daisies which will spread and spoil the grass unless checked. Even here, though, knowledge of facts alone is not enough to settle what is 'needed'. The decision to water or to apply weed-killer depends on *prior* value judgments about the desirability of daisies in lawns, or in other words about what is meant by 'spoiling the grass'. Merely to *describe* the situation could never be enough. A drug addict, to take another example, may say that he needs heroin; a doctor may say that he needs a cure. Here again 'the facts' are the same in either case. What is different is the goal or end valued by the addict and the doctor respectively. Even if we assumed that both addict and doctor knew all 'the facts' about the effects of drug-taking, until these two managed to agree in their *evaluation* of the situation, there would be no possibility of their agreeing as to what constituted the former's 'needs'.

Agreement about needs, then, depends upon agreement about values. An adolescent, you may say, needs freedom to express him-

6

self; I may say that he needs to learn to consider other people's feelings. To claim, therefore, that education should 'meet the needs' of adolescents (or of any other category of pupil), or to argue that a curriculum is a good one if it 'meets the children's needs', by itself is meaningless. 'Needs' for what? Unless goals are specified, no 'needs' can be identified. Even then, unless the goals are agreed to be good ones, 'meeting needs' is still far from being justified. A young bully, for example, from *his* point of view may 'need' to find victims. Plainly this is a 'need' which, though identifiable, should *not* be met. Further still, though, even if we agreed to deprive the bully of *some* of his 'needs', and even if we managed to reach agreement about which of his 'needs' we *would* satisfy, it would still have to be shown that it was *education*, specifically, which should be employed to bring about these deprivations and satisfactions.

It is not education, specifically, which meets the needs for example of a starving man. Why should it be assumed to be appropriate for education, then, to meet the needs of an unloved or insecure or jealous child? Even if we established that the young bully in my example needed, say, self-esteem, we would still have decided nothing as to what his needs might be in terms of *education*. A shopkeeper, a nurse, a tax inspector, a psychiatrist, all 'meet the needs' of their respective clients, but none of them necessarily do so in an 'educative' way. Even to *identify* a child's needs, then, and even to agree as to which of them are prerequisites for the achievement of *worthwhile* goals, could be only partial steps, at most, in the direction of devising a justifiable education or schooling for him.

I shall later have to take up again in more detail this question of the adequacy of needs-statements as *justifications* for doing anything. (See section 4 of chapter 2, below.) For the present it is becoming plain enough, I hope, that the notion of 'need', by itself, never adequately justifies the sending of children to school. To begin with, many educational needs-statements fail to specify any goals, and thus make it impossible in practice either to decide what the 'needs' are, or to assess whether the educational provision is satisfying them or not. Unfortunately this sort of vacuity seems most typically to be found, for example, in statements made by government-sponsored or other representative public groups with the specifically avowed aim of guiding and advising teachers. Yet, as R. F. Dearden and others have pointed out (Dearden, 1966, p. 5), either no goals are specified at all, or they are described so ambiguously that virtually anything one wished could count as a 'need' and therefore, also, as its fulfilment.

To take a more recent example than those usually cited, the Humanities Curriculum Project, too, was avowedly set up to develop a form of education which would '... meet the needs of adolescent pupils of average and below average academic ability' (quoted by Stenhouse, 1968, p. 26). But 'needs' for what? Without specifying goals, any sort of process which gained for such pupils the prerequisites for doing *anything*, could count as 'meeting their needs'. In terms of *whose* values were those employed on the research supposed to try to devise their educational programme? Of course, in undertaking the research, Stenhouse and his team have subsequently had many interesting things to say about what they believe to be the important goals which education should enable this category of pupils to achieve. But the specific thing to be discovered by the *research* was how to 'meet the needs', not how to identify the goals or ends which alone could possibly indicate *which* 'needs' to 'meet'. The directive given to the Project was thus completely empty of practical guidance.

Other sorts of educational needs-statements, by contrast, identify goals plainly enough, but fail to show what is good about them and why education, specifically, should be regarded as the means to their attainment. Frequently, for example, one hears pronouncements such as, 'Education is a national investment. If this country is to compete successfully in world markets today, it needs a highly educated labour force.' But why 'highly educated'? Why not for example 'highly trained' or 'highly skilled' or just 'technologically minded' or 'clever at overseas advertising' or 'ready to go out and sell'? Might not 'highly educated' pupils perhaps turn out inconveniently to be unwilling to regard themselves *as* 'a labour force' or to see 'successful competition' as a goal of overriding value? In the same vein one can imagine a father advising his adolescent son, 'You'll need all the education you can get, when you start looking for a job with good promotion prospects.' But again, why 'education'? Why not just 'good examination results'?

Each 'need' identified in this way generates its own brand of 'education' to serve it. Thus educational discussion today is full of such commodity-names and slogans as 'education for national progress', 'education for leisure', 'education for citizenship', 'education for healthy growth', 'education for the world of work', 'education for a good job', 'education for living', and so on. But none of these brand slogans reveal why it is education, and not some other commodity, which should be regarded as the main prerequisite for the achievement of their ends. And none of them question whether or not it is right, in the first place, to regard education merely as a commodity.

On the one hand, then, it is vacuous to talk about education as something which should meet the needs of a particular sort of child, whether 'adolescent', 'average or below average', 'superior', 'disadvantaged', 'non-academic', or anything else. Such talk, by omitting to specify goals, makes the identification of needs impossible. On the other hand, however, even when goals *are* specified and even if we agree, perhaps, that some of these goals *do* represent worthwhile goods of one sort or another, it is still uninformative to say that 'education' is whatever enables such ends to be attained, since we are left with no guidance as to how to distinguish educational from other kinds of 'need' such as physical, psychological, social, economic, political, and so on. Moreover, it is still open to question whether or not 'education' is, in this sense, a means to an end at all.

Since schooling is a social practice engaged in by individuals, 'needs' for schooling can be described either in individual or in societal terms. The two kinds of 'need' function rather differently, however, as ostensible reasons for sending children to school. In sections 2-4 of this chapter I shall look more closely at 'individual', and in section 5 at 'societal', needs. Throughout the whole discussion, though, the bulk of what I have to say will be in the form of comment upon the kind of educational guidance which is supposed to become available to teachers through the empirical study of individuals and of society. Since it is almost always assumed that the identification of 'needs' is an empirical matter independent of valuations, my examples, in other words, will for the most part have to be drawn from the writings of educational psychologists and social psychologists, regarding 'individual' needs, and of sociologists of education on 'societal' ones. I shall argue, first, that no practical guidance for teachers is forthcoming from these sciences, by themselves, since questions of value are continually begged in them; and, second, that in default of an adequate theory of value in terms of which to assess individual and societal needs, what teachers are left with is a distorted and distorting model both of the content and of the methods proper to education. The final section of the chapter will consist of a brief description of some features of this model in the form in which it may sometimes be found in practice.

2 Individual needs

In the recent past at least, perhaps the two most widely taught examples of attempts at a scientific specification of individual needs have been Havighurst's 'developmental tasks' (Havighurst, 1953) and Maslow's 'hierarchy of needs' (Maslow, 1954). In both of these one finds the three sorts of defect which I have described above, namely, vagueness about the goals for which the so-called 'needs' are said to be required, and consequently ambiguity about the nature of the 'needs' themselves, and about their relevance to education, specifically, as the means to their satisfaction.

In Havighurst's account one learns that teachers should assist primary schoolchildren to acquire, for example, the skills needed for getting along with age-mates, wholesome attitudes to self as a growing organism, and the concepts needed for daily living. In secondary school, children should acquire concepts needed for civic competence, for socially responsible behaviour, for effective use of the body ... and so on. But what exactly *is* 'civic competence', for example? What is the *right* way of 'getting along with age-mates'? What 'good' is it being assumed that we all know that we should 'effectively use' the body *for*? It seems astonishing that anyone could ever have supposed that something scientifically informative was contained in prescriptions as ambiguous as these. In practice, I think, what teachers have often taken from them has just been *carte blanche* to proceed in any way they personally happened to think 'needed'. Perhaps, indeed, this may account for the continuing popularity of Havighurst's account, since virtually anything at all which one thought good for children could on this view be dignified with the title of 'developmental task' and taught under the guise of 'meeting psychosocial needs'.

Because Havighurst's *goals* could so obviously mean vastly different things to different people, the nature of the 'need-states' postulated by him is itself equally obscure. It is never clear whether the kind of 'necessity' invoked as a basis for his 'tasks' is supposed to be physiological, logical, psychological, or anything else. For example, are we meant to think that a primary school child 'needs', say, 'concepts for daily living' in the same sense that a starving man needs food, and that the outcome for the child without his concepts will prove as dire as for the man who is left to starve? But, though we can give an adequate physiological description of the food-needs of the starving man, no such account is forthcoming in the case of the child's concepts. If, on the other hand, Havighurst's 'needs' are merely *logically* implicit, in his view, in the very nature of the children he is describing (as for example the 'need' for words of some sort is logically implicit in the 'nature' of talking, or the need for legs of some sort is 'in' the nature of walking), then he is not saying something scientifically informative at all.

In Maslow's 'hierarchy of needs', although as Dearden points out (1968, p. 16) a distinction is carefully made between 'deficit' (physiological?) and 'growth' (cultural?) needs, the same disturbing impression is conveyed that people *must* satisfy all of their 'needs' or something extremely dire will befall them, and that *what* they need is as fixed and unalterable as the physiological limits of survival. The 'need' for growth seems itself to be no more than some unexplained kind of 'deficit'. Thus, for example, Maslow writes:

> It is quite true that man lives by bread alone—when there is no bread. But what happens to man's desires when there *is* plenty of bread ... ? At once other (and 'higher') needs emerge and these, rather than physiological hungers, dominate the organism. And when these in turn are satisfied new (and still 'higher') needs emerge and so on. (1943, p. 375)

The organism is endlessly driven on. Growth 'hungers' succeed physiological 'hungers'. When one set of 'deficits' is filled up, for no particular reason at all another inexorably supervenes. The 'organism' is entirely 'dominated' by these needs. It does nothing but what it *needs must* do. Why the supervenient hungers should be called 'higher' (rather than just 'later') is never explained, nor, indeed, why any part of the whole inescapable process should be thought to have any value at all. Yet, as we have seen, the notion of 'need' is unintelligible apart from judgments of value. Man would not even bother to live 'by bread alone', if he did not think life worth living.

The notion of 'self-actualization', which Maslow later introduced into his theory in order to suggest that needs-satisfaction is somehow *bound* to produce something worthwhile ultimately, is logically redundant. If the organism is dominated by its needs in any case, then it is pointless to inquire whether needs-satisfaction is of any value or whether one need *should* be satisfied rather than another. If needs *must* be satisfied, there's no point in asking whether they *should* be. Moreover, even if such an inquiry were not beside the point, value-judgments would still be required in order to distinguish 'self-actualization' from, say, self-gratification and self-deception.

Similar problems arise when Maslow introduces the notion of 'health' to try to explain why later needs are 'higher' than earlier ones, and thus to fill the value-gap in his account. For example, he writes:

> But this is not only a series of increasing need-gratifications; it is as well a series of increasing degrees of psychological health. (1948, p. 409)

'Health', however, is itself an evaluative concept. One's view of what constitutes it is apt to change as one's values change. *Which* 'hungers' does one have to satisfy, in order to be healthy? Aren't the earlier ones (e.g. for water and warmth) just as important not only for physical but also for *psychological* health as the later ones (e.g. for Mozart or stained glass windows)? If I 'hunger' for wine, women and song, or for fish and chips on Fridays, or to be able to play all of Bach's preludes and fugues note-perfect, do all of these hungers have to be satisfied before I can be 'healthy'? *How* satisfied do they have to be—completely, or just a bit? often, or once in a while? immediately, or by the time I am sixty-five? When 'health' is *defined* as the state of affairs in which I have all the things which I need, the definition is merely circular: I am healthy when I have what I need in order to be 'healthy'. Without explaining what is *valuable* in any state of affairs called 'healthy', we have no practical means of distinguishing health from illness when we see it. Moreover, if one is only healthy when *all* one's needs have been satisfied, then we are all ill. And we are going to stay that way —for no sooner is one set of needs satisfied, than at once new hungers will emerge to dominate us.

Readers may like to examine further the shortcomings of notions such as 'health' and 'self-actualization' as justificatory concepts, by consulting for example some of R. S. Peters' work on these subjects (1964; 1966, e.g. p. 56). In the meantime, in spite of these weaknesses, needs-philosophies die hard. More sophisticated examples are all the time becoming available.

One of the most recent can be found in John P. DeCecco's *The*

Psychology of Learning and Instruction: Educational Psychology (DeCecco, 1968). The sophistication of the account, by comparison with those of Havighurst and Maslow, arises from its assimilation of recent research results into the underlying philosophical model. (For a summary of some of these results, see for example section 9 of Bindra and Stewart, 1966.) Briefly, it now appears that former descriptions of human 'needs' as arising from drives to reduce 'tensions' set up by basically physiological deficits, were incomplete. Not only, it seems, do individuals need to have tensions *reduced*, whenever they rise above a certain level. They also, apparently, 'need' to have their tensions *increased* whenever they sink below a certain point. Thus, DeCecco writes:

> The motivational image of the individual, as reflected in current research and theory, is shifting from that of a deprived individual driven to satisfy basic needs only to win a moment's peace in his long struggle for survival to that of an individual who seeks stimulation to satisfy certain expectations which arise out of his past experience and to avoid the monotony of a familiar environment. (op. cit., p. 157)

This does not mean, as at first one might think, that theorists no longer regard individuals merely as bundles of deficit-states, driven to action by their deprivations and *only* acting in order to remedy those lacks (or to 'meet needs'). Abandoning the deficit-bundle view of individuals would be tantamount to relinquishing altogether the notion that 'needs' form the ultimate basis of human action, and this, unfortunately, is not at all what DeCecco has in mind.

What he is proposing, in effect, is that a *new* 'deficit' should now be added to the original lists of 'basic' and 'growth' needs (food, shelter, esteem, and so on). Whereas previously it was thought that the 'need' to reduce stimulation and tension was the common factor in all deficit-induced action, so that action always tended to drive the organism towards the physiologically balanced state of homeostasis, now, by contrast, stimulation and tension is *itself* to be counted, according to DeCecco, as something of which individuals can have a deficit, or in other words of which they can be in a state of 'need'. Individuals, therefore, are unavoidably stimulated to seek stimulation. They 'need' to be in a constant state of need. When all of their 'deficits', seemingly, have been satisfied, they now turn out to be suffering from a 'deficit' of deficits!

We organisms are trapped, then, in an infinite regress of needs:

I need my needs ... I need to need my needs ... I need to need my need of needs ... and so on. Not surprisingly this puts the notion of 'homeostasis', too, in an equivocal position. *Is* it a state of 'satisfaction' (or, if you like, 'balance'), or isn't it? As DeCecco notes on the next page of his book:

> ... our motivational model does not require us to accept a hierarchy of needs ... For one thing such a view of need gratification is a misinterpretation of the physiological view of homeostasis, which is a dynamic and not a fixed state of physical equilibrium. (op. cit., p. 158)

The individual, then, is shuffled back and forth ('dynamic physical equilibrium') between the equally unsatisfactory limits of excitement and apathy, or of stimulation and the 'need' for stimulation. Gratification is just a sort of uneasy satiation. Enough, as William Blake once remarked, is too much.

When it comes to relating this astonishing picture of life to education, further defects become clear. Children in school, or anywhere else, are always in this view in a state of need. It is this which drives them to action, and it is only because of this that they act at all. The more need-gratifying a particular action is found by the individual to be, the more permanent his tendencies to act in that way become. This behaviour-modification in the direction of ever greater gratification is defined as 'learning'—and a prima facie connection between needs-gratification on the one hand and education, on the other, is thus established at one leap. But this is not enough. How can we be *sure* that such 'learning' will be educative? Well, says DeCecco:

> Despite the winds of controversy which sweep American education, we concur considerably on what our educational goals should be, and several groups have successfully set these down. (op. cit., p. 31)

Well done, groups! Since all the educational goals have been 'successfully set down' (dynamic intellectual equilibrium?), all that teachers have to do is to arrange school conditions so that children *can* only 'meet their needs' (e.g. for self-esteem) by performing tasks (e.g. learning to read) which serve to achieve the agreed goals.

American teachers are indeed fortunate, on this view. Since all pupil activity must, perforce, be in the direction of 'meeting needs', so long as the conditions within which pupils have to act are manipulated so that their needs *can* only be met when their actions are 'educationally' desirable, then 'education' will be virtually inevitable (for some pupils at least). By tinkering about with pupil's need-gratifications with sufficient adroitness, then, theoretically teachers could induce pupils to undertake any learning-tasks which they cared to devise. Indeed, as DeCecco explains for example on pp. 264-8, 'teaching' by definition *is* simply the intentional conditioning of pupils to seek 'educationally' desirable goals. Questions about *why* children should go to school for this treatment, or in other words why they should be 'educated', are thus merely sidestepped. They *should* be educated, it is argued, because only by pursuing 'educational goals' can they meet their needs—and 'meeting their needs' is something which they are inescapably driven to try to do. Since the 'educational goals' have been agreed upon, therefore in theory no problems remain.

But in practice, of course, the situation is quite different. The fact that the 'educator' has made the satisfaction of needs conditional upon the mastering of learning-tasks, remains unjustified. The question of the sense in which the goals *are* 'educational' ones is merely begged, by saying that they have all been agreed anyway. Moreover, the equation of teaching and learning with conditioning, upon which the connection of needs-gratification with schooling and education is ultimately made to rest, is highly questionable, to say the least.

I shall pursue the topic of the connection of 'learning' with 'conditioning' in more detail in section 4, below. Some related matters, however, such as the details of the physiological theory of homeostasis and of the psychological mechanisms of reinforcement, I must leave the reader to study elsewhere. (Short accounts by Hull, Tolman and Nissen, can be found for example in Teevan and Birney, 1964, chapters 1, 3, and 5.) An account of some of the methods by which teachers use individual need-gratification to subserve the achievement of agreed 'educational goals' will be described in section 5, below, in my commentary (pp. 27-9) on the work of Dreeben.

3   Individual needs and developmental norms

It is not only in America that needs-philosophies of education are rampant. In England, too, my impression is that they still form the received doctrine upon which the vast majority of teachers would claim to base their practice. Courses of teacher-training, for example, are still for the most part heavily weighted with studies in educational psychology and its application to 'methods of teaching', and there is a continuing bias within educational psychology itself towards needs-interpretations of human action and motivation.

The assumption seems to be that the more we know about the psychological development of children, the better—automatically, or without further serious reflection—we will understand what they need for their education. But this would only be true, or would only stand a chance of being true, if children were like, say, machines or plants or something whose efficient functioning or 'healthy' development were matters determinable by reference to fairly rigid, settled standards and criteria of value. In that case, plainly, the more 'facts' we knew about how the machine worked or the plant grew, the 'better' we would be able to look after and control it. But whereas machines and plants do not themselves have a sense of values, children do. Children are not merely things *of* more or less value, as machines and plants are. They themselves *put* more or less value on things.

Similarly, a child's education is not merely something which looks after him while he produces a more or less valuable product such as could be got from a machine, or a more or less valuable crop such as could be taken from a healthy plant. His education contributes to *his* judgments of value. This is not something which is brought about merely by 'meeting his needs', whether they were 'healthy' ones, or promoted his 'healthy' development, or not. On the contrary, without some sort of educated sense of values it would not be possible in the first place to make judgments as to what the 'needs' were. 'Needs' have no existence, in abstraction from the valuation of goals. To say that something 'meets a need', individual or societal, *raises*, rather than settles, questions as to its value. Moreover, even if its value for individual or societal survival were agreed, its *educational* value would be another question altogether.

It is true that many educational and social psychologists nowadays, very conscious of the kind of criticisms which I have been sketching above, are careful to try to detach their investigations of matters of 'fact' about children and their 'needs' from questions about the *value* of different forms of needs-satisfaction and about the relative value of different needs. The point has now been made many times, that '... we cannot infer a duty to teach in some particular way from the descriptive sentences of psychology' (Best, 1962, p. 7). This distinction, however, between the states of affairs which we judge 'in fact' to exist and those which we judge that it would be of *value* to achieve, is by no means a simple one (see, for example, Hudson, 1969). And, when drawn by psychologists in an oversimplified way, the result very often is merely to cut psychology adrift from education altogether, the one entirely surrounded by 'facts', the other by 'values'.

Margaret Clark (1967), for instance, writes:

> The role of the teacher and the function of education are basically important issues which should be considered by any teacher in training. Such issues are, however, not within the remit of the psychologist. The psychologist is concerned with 'what is' and not 'what ought to be'. (pp. 154-5)

What, then, can an 'educational' psychologist be concerned with? In spite of all disclaimers, whenever psychology is 'applied' to education, value-assumptions are made. Even to say that it is not the business of psychologists to *prescribe* what teachers ought to do, but just to *describe* what is liable to happen when they do it, is still to assume that psychologists somehow know what 'it' is, which it is their proper business to describe. The 'role of the psychologist' is *itself*, in common with other 'roles', not just a matter of 'what is' but also of 'what ought to be'. 'Facts' and 'values' cannot be simply wrenched apart in this way. Without value-assumptions one would not even know that it was one's business to look at the facts.

Let me give another example of this illusory division and recombination of roles. The social psychologist K. M. Evans, in her book on *Attitudes and Interests in Education* (1965), explains early on that of course it is not for psychologists to decide *which* attitudes and interests 'educators' should know how to develop in children. Accordingly, when the question later arises as to how in that case she managed to decide which attitudes, interests and modes of development she ought to study in her book, the answer which she gives is that this is just a matter of one's 'philosophical' preferences:

> To legislate for the education of children is a group responsibility and a task which should not be approached lightly. In what ways is it good, for them and for society, that they should develop ... ? The ... question is really philosophical, and we are all philosophers enough to be able to attempt to answer it. (op. cit., p. 142)

Thus, she adds:

> ... the author has made philosophical decisions about what
> attitudes and experiments are educationally important. Even
> psychologists are people and have their predilections. (p. 143)

When psychologists tell us what our 'developmental needs' are,
then, it seems inevitable that their advice to us will be strongly
coloured by their personal philosophy or 'predilections'. Yet, on the
other hand, if they are utterly 'scientific' and keep their 'predilections' right out of their picture of 'the facts', it would be impossible
for them to explain what the point of *our* looking at 'the facts'
could possibly be.

It is no answer to this problem to say, as is most usually said,
that psychologists are not trying to prescribe the needs of any
particular child, but are merely describing what is needed by
'children in general'. Developmental norms, or pictures of the stages
through which the emotional, social, intellectual, moral and other
aspects of children's lives 'generally' develop, are themselves
prescriptive, not descriptive. There are no general *laws* of human
development in the sense in which there are 'laws' which allow us
to predict, say, the movements of material bodies—since what is
to count *as* 'development' and *as* 'human' are themselves evaluative
and not just descriptive notions.

At most, 'developmental norms' indicate some of the typical
'needs' of typical children as judged by typical or consensual standards of value. In practice, therefore, they provide no more than
the roughest guidance for teachers trying to work in highly indi-
vidualized, personal relationships with particular children. Indeed,
they may as often prove misleading, I would think, as helpful, since
the values built into them could well be quite extraneous to the
values arising from the teacher's relationships with this or that individual child. Such norms, in other words, can as easily distort, as
guide, a teacher's decisions as to what he should do in a particular
case, making him liable to act in such a way as to make the norms,
as it were, come true. The norms are no *substitute* for personal
decision and judgment—indeed, they are themselves a generalized
outcome of it. The most that they can do is to suggest a range of
possible alternatives from which a teacher might be wise to choose.
To be able to understand *only* what is 'normal', however, must at
times be as much a handicap as a help to a teacher.

Leaving college, equipped let us say with a good knowledge of developmental norms, a teacher is confronted by particular children each with his own particular sense of values and each, therefore, with particular individual needs and ways of behaving. It is quite impossible for that teacher either to understand those children's values or to predict what they will be likely to do to preserve and promote them, if the main part of what he is relying on in the way of 'theory' is his generalized knowledge of some of the sorts of things which 'children in general' value and do. One can say that 'children generally' need security, self-esteem, affection, and so on, or that at various ages and stages they will need to appear rebellious or to make strong positive identifications, to become more independent or to form close peer-group relationships, to have plenty of conversation with adults or to have plenty of non-verbal 'concrete experiences' ... and so on. But exactly *which* of all these things they will need, and when and why, and of what quality, and whether they should be given them without further ado or should have to work for them, and in what sort of context they will recognize, or appreciate, or accept, or value them, when they get them—these are problems of vital importance, about which *in practice* a teacher will be making decisions every moment of the day, and over the surface of which his mere knowledge of general norms will slip with almost total superficiality.

Developmental norms can tell us only what things a child of a certain sort *may* need, *if* it is assumed also that it would be valuable for him to develop in a certain direction. They cannot tell us *which* sort of child this or that one is, nor distinguish for us the directions in which he should move. A particular child's actions can only be understood in the context of what he personally *intends* or *means* them to be. What he intends or means is in turn something which we can only fathom to the extent that we gain knowledge, not just of 'children in general' and *their* needs, but of the values of this particular child.

My contention here, that not even someone's *actions* (let alone his needs for action) can be identified without reference to his intentions, purposes and values, raises once again wider philosophical issues concerning the explanation of human action. The topic may be explored further by reading, for example, A. I. Melden's *Free Action* (1961, especially chapter 3). In the meantime, to return to the example with which I opened this chapter, I hope that it is clear at least that while we may say that *if* someone means or wants to play patience *then* he will need a pack of cards, nevertheless, from the observable fact of his getting out a pack of cards we cannot infer anything in particular about the game that he means or wants to play. He might not even be intending to play a card game, but just, say, to check that the pack is complete, or to compare the designs of the kings of the four suits, or to build himself a house out of cards, or to practise flicking a thin piece of card across the room, or simply to begin tidying-up the drawer in which the cards are kept. Similarly, from the fact that statistically significant samples of children *act* in certain ways at certain ages and stages, nothing in *particular* can be inferred about the significance of this or that action. Behavioural norms do not explain action: they themselves need explaining.

It seems therefore totally misleading to write, as Margaret Clark does, that:

> With our present level of knowledge it is sometimes only possible to predict the likely outcomes of a series of actions, rather than to state with absolute certainty the inevitable consequences of certain environmental variables. (op. cit., p. 140)

Quite clearly the implication here is that it is only a matter of time before all the variables will have been discovered and psychologists will thus be able to 'state with absolute certainty the inevitable consequences' of them in terms of predictions about children's behaviour. But there will never be *more* than 'likely' outcomes to situations in which human beings are involved. Action is not the 'inevitable consequence' of *anything*, since in part at least it is always undertaken with particular values, purposes and intentions in mind. The sort of deterministic psychology which assumes that actions involving people are no different in kind (but only in complexity) from happenings involving material bodies, will never provide educational and practical guidance in classroom decisions involving particular children. The most important feature of human behaviour—namely, that it is meaningless apart from the values for the sake of which it is undertaken—will be the very feature of which such a psychology will never be able to take proper account.

4 Individual needs and learning

Thus far I have argued that there is nothing unambiguously 'good' about 'meeting children's needs', even when they are said to be developmentally 'normal' ones, and even when conditions of life at school and elsewhere are so arranged that needs *can* only be met when individuals perform 'educationally desirable' tasks. This latter strategy, which in its extreme form involves the reduction of 'learning' and 'teaching' to conditioning, raises additional difficulties, moreover, to some account of which I must now turn. In this section, then, I shall argue that there are important differences between 'teaching' and 'learning' on the one hand and 'conditioning' on the other, and also that if 'education' were no more than socially approved conditioning there would be no point in asking why children *should* go to school.

Individual needs are usually thought of as a sort of driving force or motivating condition which can be activated by presenting an appropriate stimulus or incentive to the individual. Hunger, for example, is one such drive or motivating force. The presentation of food acts as a stimulus or incentive to the hungry individual to spring into action appropriate to the satisfaction of his need for food, or if you like appropriate to the relief of the tensions brought about by his hunger plus the sight of food. Now I hope that I have said enough already to suggest that what is here called a 'need for food' is not *just* an empirically observable 'fact' but something which can only be identified in the context of an evaluation of the whole state of affairs of which it is a part. This is as true, I think, in the case of so-called 'basic' or 'deficit' needs such as food as it is in the case of 'cultural' or 'growth' needs such as esteem and independence. What 'drives' the individual, whether it is food or independence that he is seeking, is not his 'needs' but his sense of what is important and valuable. It is *from* his evaluations that his 'needs' derive, not vice versa. A hunger-striker, though hungry enough, would not agree that *food* was his 'basic need'.

Nevertheless, to a psychologist who starts from the assumption that people only act when they are driven to and that what drives them to act is their needs, it follows that 'learning' is merely the set of behavioural changes which an organism makes in order to adjust to emerging environmental conditions of needs-supply. In other words, as DeCecco puts it, learning is:

> ... a relatively permanent change in a behavioral tendency and is the result of reinforced practice. The reinforced practice ... is the cause of the learning. (op. cit., p. 243)

The 'reinforcement' referred to here is the gratification of a need. In effect what DeCecco is saying, then, is that by manipulating the conditions under which children can secure need-gratifications one can bring about behaviour changes, in the same sort of way that by manipulating the supply of carrots one can modify the behaviour of donkeys. If the manipulated conditions are relatively regular— if the carrots are regularly given, or withheld, for certain bits of behaviour—then the modifications in behaviour will become relatively permanent. The manipulations, on this view, constitute 'teaching'; the modifications constitute 'learning'. *Any* modifications could be demanded, and, so long as living conditions at school (and, as far as possible, at home and everywhere else) were consistently arranged so that needs could only be gratified upon production of those modifications in behaviour, *some* children at least would manage the task. In *theory*, then, the modifications which could count as 'education' are entirely open to anyone to decide, upon any grounds he chose. In practice, as we have seen, several groups of American educators have shown us that there is no need to take a decision at all.

But, in addition to the confusion involved here in taking 'needs', rather than valuations, as the 'driving force' behind behavioural change (in many ways, one could say, it is the behaviour of the donkey which 'educates' his master, rather than vice versa; the master merely makes the donkey work), there are several further points at which the above model of teaching, learning and education is inadequate.

First, an essential feature of successful conditioning is the *regularity* with which the behaviour to be 'learned' is reinforced, and with which other behaviour receives negative reinforcement. Now a relatively permanent response to *regularity* is not one which could *itself* be acquired by conditioning, since successful conditioning depends *upon* it. Unless, then, the animal (or child or whatever is being conditioned) has *already* learned to distinguish 'regular' from 'irregular' conditions, the whole process could not even get started. Or, if it could, then *how* it started would be inexplicable. Theories of conditioning, therefore, far from 'explaining' learning, seem to require an account of 'learning' in order to explain *them*. Learning (or at least some learning) involves getting to see a meaning or significance or import in some area of one's experience. Without this dawning grasp of the pattern of events, their 'regularity' or 'irregularity' would simply make no impression. Since the success of conditioning depends upon this 'regularity', some learning can explain conditioning, but no conditioning can account for learning.

Second, and rather similarly, if 'teaching' involves something to do with trying to *show* someone the significance or import of some feature of their experience, although this could account for someone's learning something and, therefore, could account for his becoming conditioned to expect certain reinforcements to be regularly associated with certain kinds of behaviour, the conditioning itself could never *be* the same thing as the teaching, any more than it could be the same thing as the learning. Any behaviour, theoretically, could be associated by conditioning with the receipt of positive reinforcements. For instance, one could set out to condition children to wiggle their ears whenever the headmaster entered the classroom, by regularly rewarding those who managed to do so and penalizing those who did not—or in other words, as DeCecco puts it, by 'reinforced practice'. Only some children would ever master the task, just as only some children ever manage to master other tasks set in school. The point, however, is that not even those who did become successfully conditioned would have been taught to do so *by the reinforced practice*. They would first have had to learn to see the whole process as 'practising' the mastery of a certain task. The practice *itself* would not enable them to do this, since it would merely be practice of the task—not practice in seeing repeated attempts at the task as 'practice'.

Moreover, merely being rewarded whenever they wiggled their ears at the right time, although it would be nice for them, would not itself teach them what 'the right time' was. However often they did the right thing at the right time by chance, and were rewarded, and however *desirable* it therefore became to them to do it again, doing the right thing at the right time would still be a matter of chance, unless they had managed to grasp what 'the right time' meant. The desirability of something does not increase the likelihood of its happening by chance, nor does it show why it happens or, in other words, what there is about it, logically, which makes sense of its happening when it does. One could be conditioned, then, to expect a reward if one wiggled at the right time. But one could not be conditioned to *recognize* 'the right time'. This is something which one would have to learn, and which one could possibly be taught.

Third, both teaching and learning are activities which are only identifiable by reason of their intrinsic point, or, to put it another way, because there is some intelligible reason for undertaking them. Like 'needing', they are *not* identifiable or recognizable because of their empirical features alone. Just as one cannot recognize that someone is engaging in an activity 'because he needs to', merely by observing him, nor identify an action as a 'needful' one merely by checking its empirical features against some fixed or standard pattern for 'needful' actions in general, so, also, there is no standard list of actions which *must* be performed when one is 'teaching' or when one is 'learning' and which make those activities recognizable. Only when observable actions intelligibly exemplify the logical *point* of 'teaching' and 'learning', can they be identified *as* actions within the overall 'activities' of teaching and learning (see Langford, 1968, p. 117). By contrast, conditioning and being conditioned by definition *are* processes identifiable solely by their observable features—since the only features of anything which theorists of conditioning will admit to exist *are* the empirically observable ones. Therefore there *is* a fixed or standard list of empirical features by means of which (in theory at least) 'conditioning' processes may be recognized. Further, it follows that there is no *intrinsic* point to conditioning. What is being associated with what, in a conditioning situation, is of no logical consequence whatever. It simply does not matter. One could (in theory) be conditioned to do *anything*, without this making any difference to the fact that what was happening to one *was* that one was 'being conditioned'.

The point of 'teaching', plainly enough, is to try to bring about learning; but this, as we have seen, is not at all the same thing as trying to bring about a change of behaviour or belief, although of course it may have those consequences as well. Again, the point of 'learning' (if one can speak of so complex a thing as having 'a' point) is to try to understand how to act or how to interpret one's experience in a meaningful way; but this, too, is not at all the same sort of thing as merely *undergoing* a fairly permanent change in one's behaviour or in the state of one's mind. By contrast, the only point of 'conditioning', from the conditioner's point of view, is whatever good or bad ends the process is being employed as a means to, and, from the conditionee's point of view, whatever 'positive reinforcements' he can manage to get out of it. Both of these 'points' are *extrinsic*, in other words, to the process itself. In itself, any particular example of the process could be both a genuine example of 'conditioning' and yet also intrinsically pointless. 'Intrinsically pointless teaching' and 'intrinsically pointless learning', however, are self-contradictory notions. If there were nothing intelligible to understand, one could not conceivably 'learn' it. And if one were trying to get someone to do something entirely unintelligible to you both, one could not possibly be 'teaching' him.

To sum up, then, of course one can *change* someone's behaviour by changing the environmental conditions surrounding him, and if, for example, one *regularly* gives him a team point or a gold star when he writes a complete sentence or adds up numbers correctly, then the change in his behaviour may possibly become quite permanent. In the very general sense, too, that such behavioural changes were not due solely to maturation, I suppose that one could call the changes 'learning' and the process of inducing them 'teaching'. Philosophers of education, however, such as Scheffler (1965, chapters 1 and 5) and Langford (1968, chapters 6-8), would argue that both 'teaching' and 'learning' involve, centrally, some reference to the meaningfulness, or rationality, or perhaps intelligibility, of the *content* of what is being 'taught' and 'learned'. 'Teaching' and 'learning' in this sense cannot be accounted for in terms of conditioning, since their content is as important as the observable methods which they employ. Indeed, it seems unlikely that 'conditioning' itself can be accounted for, without reference to 'teaching' and 'learning' in a more restricted sense. Pupils could be conditioned to expect rewards for certain kinds of behaviour, but it is hard to see how the acquisition of the ability to behave in those ways could itself be intelligible, by reference to the process of conditioning alone.

For these sorts of reasons, then, there are serious theoretical difficulties involved in the reduction of 'teaching' and 'learning' to 'conditioning' which is required by the value-gap in needs-based philosophies of education. But even if teaching and learning *were* no more than socially approved conditioning, there would still be the *practical* problem of deciding which goals should be approved. The pupils' 'needs' could provide no scientific or other pointer to guide such a decision, since, as we have seen, the existence of 'needs' itself *presupposes* the existence of acceptable standards of value. One would be arguing in a circle if one said that the 'agreed goals' were good because children 'needed' them—since one could only decide that the children 'needed' them if one had *already* agreed that they were good.

An apparent way out of this logical circularity or impasse is to argue that what the children 'really' need is what meets the needs of *society*. In other words, the claim may now be made that the 'true' guide in the diagnosis of *individual* need is *societal* need.

'The needs of society' on this view are the *same* (but writ large, as it were) as the 'real' needs of its individuals. Let us look at some examples of what is meant by 'societal needs' and the 'meeting' of them, therefore, in order to see what sort of solution they are claimed to provide to the problems raised.

5 Societal needs

In the sort of needs-philosophy which we are now going to consider, individual needs and drives are supposed to account for the *motivational* side of what goes on in schools. In other words, they are held to explain why individuals act at all. Their actions are only *justified*, however, when at the same time as meeting the individual needs of the pupils concerned they *also* subserve societal ends. Only when the child is being conditioned or 'taught' to adopt societally needed ways of gratifying his individual needs, can he be said to be receiving a 'good' schooling, or in other words an 'education'. His going to school is justified, then, because it 'meets societal needs'. 'Schooling', when it conditions children to perform tasks which promote societal goals, is 'education'.

This partnership between individual and societal needs (and thus between individual and societal values) is at best an uneasy one. In practice, as we all know well, the two sets of needs are continually liable to conflict. As some sociologists speak of it, the conflict is explicit and unavoidable, as in the conflict model of schooling of which Waller's *The Sociology of Teaching* (1932) is the classic description. Thus, writes Waller:

> Typically the school is organized on some variant of the autocratic principle ... the social necessity of subordination is a condition of human achievement, and the general tradition governing the attitudes of students and teachers toward each other, set the limits of variation. (1965 edition, pp. 8-9)

Societal needs, in this model, are explicit and always override individual needs.

For other sociologists, as for Erving Goffman in *Asylums* (1961), the conflict between institutions and individuals is no less unavoidable and ultimate, but the individual (whether staff or inmate, employer or employee) is often largely unaware of the significance of the ways in which society is shaping him to its needs. The model here is conspiratorial.

In the book which I have mentioned, Goffman is writing mainly of adults in what he calls 'total institutions', that is, places such as those asylums, prisons, ships at sea, military or religious academies, concentration camps, isolation hospitals, boarding schools, residential colleges of education, and so on, in which individuals can be more or less 'totally' immured from their former selves. As he says, 'Total institutions are fateful for the inmate's civilian self ...' (1968 edition, p. 50). In the same way, schools, to the extent that they institutionalize inmates by valuing societal and devaluing individual needs, are fateful, we may conclude, for the self which each child first presents in school. The new language which he must learn, symbolic of the new attitudes which he must learn to adopt to adults ('Miss' and 'Sir'), the new goals ('stars', 'ticks'), the new ways of getting or not getting about ('in twos', 'when I say so', 'at the double'), new space for living ('my desk', 'my classroom'), new time ('maths time', 'play time', 'home time') and so on, stress to the child the nature of the norms which he is to adopt. The point is not that this may in particular cases seem to be either a good or a bad thing, but that on the conspiratorial model of norm-acquisition which Goffman describes, it is never the value to individuals, but always the value in terms of the upkeep of the institution, which is the operative reason for the 'need' to adopt the norms. In the end, 'the institution' represents the collective features of all institutions; in other words, it represents 'society'. Its 'needs', theoretically, are 'the needs of society'.

As applied to schooling today, these two models perhaps represent extreme positions. To what extent, as teachers, we are engaged in a conflict or a conspiracy on behalf of societal values, is something which we ourselves must decide. The problem, however, in so far as we are hoping to look to theory to guide us in our decisions, is that so long as theory is needs-based there seems very little chance of its offering us any radically different sort of model.

Consider, for instance, one of the most convincing recent sociological accounts of schooling, which is to be found in Robert Dreeben's On What Is Learned In School (1968). Here, the question scarcely arises as to whether or not schooling is valuable. The book is an account of what just happens to children, as a result of their going to school. Briefly, they 'acquire' societal norms. In chapter 5, for example, Dreeben explains how children learn specifically (1) to act independently rather than co-operatively, (2) to try to come up to certain standards of excellence which are identical for all,

(3) to regard themselves primarily as members of classes or *types* of person, rather than *as* persons, and (4) to value the type-casting features of themselves and to devalue the rest. The purposes behind the setting up of the conditions for the acquisition of these norms (i.e. the setting up of schools) are of course societal, not personal. The first norm is 'needed' societally because adult workers and citizens must be able to take many sorts of decision by themselves, regardless of others. That is, the need to make a decision (e.g. as an employer, as a striker, as a soldier, as a motorist) overrides the value of considering the interests of others. Similarly, the other three norms are prerequisites for the rating of individuals for the purpose of giving calculated economic rewards for work done.

The school's job, then, is to produce belief in the value of these norms—these are the 'educational goals'. The 'method' employed is of course to make use of the child's current individual needs (for security, esteem and so forth), withholding gratification of these until the child appears to be 'learning' to view the world (and himself) in the required 'adult' fashion. Principally, Dreeben says, it is the child's self-esteem (his image of an adequate, successful self) which is made to depend upon his adopting the new role. Through a variety of 'socializing' situations, such as public questioning and testing in front of his peers, various forms of competitive self-assessment, and ritualized examination procedures which reward 'independent' effort and punish co-operation as 'cheating', the child is slowly but unavoidably shamed into adulthood. Unfortunately, as Dreeben points out at the end of his description of this process:

> ... the same activities and sanctions from which some pupils derive gratification and enhancement of self-respect ... may create experiences that threaten the self-respect of others. Potentialities for success *and* failure are inherent in the tasks performed according to achievement criteria [norm (2)]. Independence [norm (1)] manifests itself as competence and autonomy in some, but as a heavy burden of responsibility and inadequacy in others. Universalistic treatment [norm (3)] represents fairness for some, cold impersonality to others. Specificity [norm (4)] may be seen as situational relevance or personal neglect. (op. cit., p. 84)

Failure, in such a situation, is not just a risk; it is a certainty (see for example the vivid accounts of this in the writings of John Holt, 1964). The 'educational methods' could not work at all (for some), unless there were actual failures as well as successes. The effective point of the methods *is* to promise success, and therefore to threaten failure.

Dreeben gives a similar warning again, two pages later, by reminding us of the logical circumstance that if psychological 'health' is dependent upon the satisfaction of needs, then in a needs-based system of schooling there cannot be anyone who is not at all times more or less psychologically 'ill'. Nevertheless, whether it is *right* that children (or anyone) in this way should be stripped of what *they* value in order to be clothed in what *we* value—and whether, indeed, even *we* value it, when we see its true colours— is not what is at issue in the book. Dreeben does not claim to be describing anything *valuable*. He does not for example name the process 'moral education'—but merely 'the acquisition of norms'. From his account of the way in which the norms are acquired, however, it is plain that the whole process involves the destruction, not the development, of values. The children change (if they're lucky enough to be able to) because they *have* to, to keep their self-respect. They acquire, not a more educated sense of values, but just a temporarily useful set of norms. The manipulative psycho-social mechanisms employed are fundamentally the same as those which for example DeCecco described as 'learning' and 'teaching' or which K. M. Evans calls 'attitude change'. But whereas Dreeben refers to the process, when it occurs in schools, simply as 'schooling', DeCecco and Evans call it 'education', thus making assumptions about the value of the process which Dreeben is careful to avoid.

Dreeben's accuracy is exceptional. Most sociologists who stress societal needs refer to the process of meeting them as 'education'. The individual is said only to be able to develop 'healthily' if he satisfies his individual need to fit securely into the pattern set by the rules and practices of his society. Alternatively he is said to be 'deprived' and 'disadvantaged' (and socially and economically, of course, he *is*), if he lacks the sort of 'education' which societally is claimed to be desirable. D. F. Swift, for example, in chapter 5 of his *Sociology of Education* (1969), describes these 'educational' (i.e., societal) goals as being (1) to inculcate the values and standards of society, (2) to maintain social solidarity, (3) to transmit the knowledge which makes up the social heritage, and (4) to develop more of such knowledge (p. 91). Thus, just as on the one hand we find 'education' described as something of utility to the individual in terms of ambiguously 'good' goals such as healthy growth, self-realization, personal freedom, socialization, etc., so on the other hand we find it declared to be equally 'good' for society, in terms equally ambiguous, such as social stability, social continuity, social innovation . . . and so on.

F. W. Garforth once stated this philosophy with great explicitness:

> We must be clear . . . that education is essentially instrumental; it is not an end in itself, as is sometimes loosely said, but a means both to fulfilment in the individual and to stability and progress in society. It is a tool . . . to achieve the aims which society sets before itself. (1964, p. 25)

In terms of the possible achievement of something valuable, such an 'education' as this is entirely empty, since there is nothing in it which is valued *for* its intrinsic worth. Not only is each set of goals (the individual and the societal) liable to cancel out the other—as, for example, societal 'solidarity' is liable to obliterate particular or individual sub-cultures. Within itself, too, each set of goals is in fact self-cancelling, as for example 'innovation' cancels 'continuity' or 'knowledge' cancels 'inculcation', and as what is 'personal' is cancelled by what is merely 'selfish' or what is 'healthy' by what is merely 'socializing'. There is no principled guidance here for the resolution of the conflict situations which the theory makes in practice inevitable, and no reasonable answer, therefore, to the basic question Why *should* children be schooled? What is good about the 'need' to go to school, remains unexplained.

Just as one does not always value what one needs, so, as for example Barry points out (1965, p. 48n.), one does not always *deserve* it either. In practical situations where one 'need' seems to conflict with another, it is impossible to decide on the basis of *need* alone what should be done, since one has not yet clarified the *valuable* features of the respective goals of the conflicting needs, and thus one cannot judge in a reasonable manner which one should be sacrificed for the sake of the greater value which might come of the other. Like rival trade unions 'needs' starkly face 'needs', and the weaker go to the wall. What is good about the goals of *both*, and the valuable respect, therefore, in terms of which the relative instrumental worth of *each* might be assessed, remains mysterious. It could only be, however, for the sake of values *shared*, not for the sake of those 'needed' as though by rival business competitors, that children should go to school.

6   Needs-based schooling

When school is seen merely as a place to which children need to go to get 'good' things which lie *outside* the process of schooling itself, then one can never explain why it is to *school* that they should go, rather than some other place; nor why, at school, it should be one task, rather than any other, upon which they should concentrate. If, for example, the 'goods' could be more easily obtained by buying them, inheriting them, stealing them, or finding them in the street, why bother with *school* as the means to their acquisition? One might just as easily win them on the pools. Similarly, in needs-based schools we make a child's security, his self-esteem, his socialization and so on, conditional upon his performing tasks such as writing compositions, solving equations, studying Shakespeare, because these are the sorts of things whose chief value, we declare, will accrue to him *later*, when he grows up, becomes adult, starts working, has leisure time to fill, and so on. But the value of his security, self-esteem and socialization *now* is not the same as the value which may accrue *later* to his being able to write compositions and solve equations, and furnishes therefore no good reason for saying that he should do the latter things *now* in ways which gain him our praise. Unless we can establish intelligible links between what is good about self-esteem and what is good about writing compositions in praiseworthy ways here and now, then the school task is nothing but an indifferent means to an end whose value may never be known.

Yet this needs-philosophy is widespread. For example, when teachers sometimes say that it is good policy to 'get children interested', in practice what this often seems to mean is that they believe that school is 'in the children's interest', or in other words is something which children 'need'. Therefore, from the teacher's point of view it follows, the children jolly well *should* 'be interested' in school; they should be *made* to 'feel their need'.

Quite often such teachers might call themselves 'progressive', because they say that they are basing schooling 'on the children's interests'. Any enterprise at all *can* be called 'progressive', in respect of its 'progress' towards its own particular set of goals, as Brauner and Burns have pointed out in this connection (1965, chapter 3). But where the goals themselves are just the traditional ones associated with schooling by custom and precedent, the 'progressive' label can be extremely misleading. It refers neither to the goals nor to the content of the schooling, but merely to its methods and manner; and even these are misconceived in ways which I have tried to describe in sections 2 and 3 above. Such teachers may be prepared in their methods and manner to 'consider children's interests' so far as those interests happen to be compatible with what the teachers judge to be the children's 'needs'. Where unhappily they are not obviously compatible, however, the teacher has no idea in his mind of revising the *content* of his notions of what the children 'need'. On the contrary the *most* that he will do, by way of adapting the content, is to 'prepare an environment' in which in fact the *same* fixed content is dressed up in all sorts of extraneously 'interesting' ways. 'Traditionalists', naturally, scorn such devices and contrivances. 'Why take all this trouble,' they say, 'just to *avoid* trouble? The children have to come to school in any case, whether they find it interesting or not; so why trouble to dress it up in fancy colours or tell it with funny stories merely to make it *seem* interesting? You may catch their attention for a while, but their interest won't last. Anyway, once they have left school, no one will be bothered much with whether they're interested in their work or not. They'll soon learn which side their bread's buttered. Making everything pleasurable now, is not only a waste of time and energy; it's a poor preparation for life.'

Personally I have more sympathy with the 'traditionalist' than with the 'progressive' here, but in neither's mind is there any notion of what could be valuable *in* the child's life here and now, and therefore of intrinsic value in his curriculum. To both, school represents a prerequisite for living, not *itself* a kind of living, too. To both, schooling is the process of making children more as they should be, according to adult norms; or more as they *need* to be, if they are to live comfortably (as it is assumed that they should) within the settled pattern of those norms. What the children themselves think about schooling, affects only how they co-operate (or don't co-operate) with their teachers. Their own valuations, in other words, are important only from the motivational point of view; they have no direct bearing on the values presupposed by the norms. The curriculum planners take for granted, then, that when the children 'grow up' they will see the point of the life which it has already been settled that their schooling will secure for them, or at least for those of them who are successful at it. All that they have to do is to get properly schooled. They will then *be* what it has been planned that they should be. The value-hypothesis will be self-confirming. In the meantime, despite any apparent lack of value in their schooling, they can rest assured that it is something entirely necessary for them if they are ever to reach (as of course few of them in fact ever will) the ideally looked-for life in which at last they will be able to start living 'properly'. But whatever would that 'ideal' life be like? Certainly there would be nothing left in it to live *for*. If there *were* still something, then this would indicate simply the continuing existence of a 'need', lurking somewhere still unsatisfied. They would have to go back to school, then, to have it dealt with.

The children's own interests have nothing to do with the value of needs-based schooling, and their motivation merely affects, as DeCecco says, their 'vim and vigor' (op. cit., chapter 5: 'Motivation: How to Increase Student Vim and Vigor'). Within the limits of their ability and self-confidence, donkeys can be induced to pull virtually any load up the hill, but they exert themselves not for the sake of the load (which is not what interests them), but for the carrots. In the same way schoolwork becomes drudgery, or, in A. C. MacIntyre's description, '... a chain of activity in which everything is done for the sake of something else and nothing for its own sake' (MacIntyre, 1964). By submitting to the school's prescriptions to 'do' this subject and 'take' that one, in accordance with their normatively predicted future 'good', children's entire perspectives upon life become progressively altered. When (or if) they emerge successfully at the other end of the process, 'schooled', they will now, to public appearance at least, have become fully predictable, fully usable and load-bearing individuals, always acting from interest, even if never with it. And their schools, like the total institutions described by Goffman (op. cit., p. 22), will have become indeed '... forcing houses for changing persons'.

All needs-based 'education' is 'compensatory', rather than of intrinsic value. It starts by diagnosing what the children have *not* got, and then sets out to make up their deficiencies, rather than to try to help them to realize the possibilities of value inherent in what they *have* already. Especially when the term 'compensatory education' is selectively applied, as at present, to groups of children regarded as being *particularly* lacking or deficient, then, as Bernstein has written (1970), this implies:

> ... that something is lacking in the family, and so in the child ... and the children are looked at as deficit systems. If only the parents were interested in the goodies we offer, if only they were

like middle-class parents, then we could do our job ... If children are labelled 'culturally deprived', then it follows that the parents are inadequate, the spontaneous realizations of their culture, its images and symbolic representations are of reduced value and significance. Teachers will have lower expectations of the children, which the children will undoubtedly fulfil. All that informs the child, that gives meaning and purpose to him outside of the school, ceases to be valid and accorded significance and opportunity for enhancement within the school. (pp. 112-13)

'This may mean,' Bernstein continues, 'that the *contents* of the learning in school should be drawn much more from the child's experience in his family and community' (p. 113). And he concludes:

We should start knowing that the social experience the child already possesses is valid and significant, and that this social experience should be reflected back to him as being valid and significant. It can only be reflected back to him if it is part of the texture of the learning experience we create. (p. 121)

But this is true not just for some children and for some learning but for all, if schooling is to be in any way educative.

Children today are increasingly disinclined to be manipulated by hope and fear (carrots and sticks) into doing blindly what adults tell them that they 'need' to do. Their advertisement-ridden daily life is already so full of professionally contrived stimuli and inducements to 'do' this or 'take' that, that they are increasingly less likely to be provoked into 'desirable' behaviour in school by offers of 'goods' whose nature is extraneous to '... the texture of the learning experience we create'. Nor are they likely to be 'started off' or 'got going' in this way upon activities whose value and point are as obscure as that of, say, 'research' into a local neighbourhood in which *they* have lived all their lives but about which their teacher plainly knows next to nothing. Unless children are asleep, under hypnosis or in a state of shock, it is one of the most obvious facts about them that they are always both 'started' and 'going' already. The *educative* task of teachers is not to give them a series of shocks followed by motivational pushes and pulls in directions alien to their own, but to try to help them to see the significance of goals which already they find interesting and take to be of some possible value. Making use of a child's interest as a means to some extrinsic end never reveals what that interest itself is worth in terms of human feeling, but devalues it by treating it as no more than a prerequisite for something else. Of course it is true that society, if it is to continue in its present direction of growth, 'needs' skilled manpower, law-abiding citizens and so on. It is true, too, that schooling may be as efficient a way as any of 'meeting these needs', in the short run at least. Certainly it is such 'schooling' which governments and local authorities want, and which they are prepared to pay for. My concern, however, has been to show that such 'schooling' is not 'education', or that its value, far from being *shown* by describing it as being 'needed', is thereby *presupposed*. When, therefore, such documents as the Spens Report, for example, advise us that '... before everything else the school should provide for the pre-adolescent and adolescent years a life which answers to their special needs' (quoted by Gribble, 1969, p. 80), not only is no guidance about 'schooling' contained in such a tautology. As an authoritative statement about the *kind* of values to be sought in education, its terminology is extremely misleading.

Not all 'individual needs' *should* be gratified. How are we to decide which should and which should not? By reference to 'societal needs'? But, similarly, not all 'societal needs' should be satisfied. How are we to decide which of them should be 'answered' and which should not? There is no way out of this impasse. Once we have equated 'schooling' with 'education', and thus reduced 'teaching' and 'learning' to the kind of person-processing which goes on in what Goffman has called the work of 'the tinkering trades' (1961, final essay), we have generated insoluble moral and practical problems for teachers and children in schools. Tinkering is a way of 'servicing' people by seeing to their 'needs', on the analogy of mechanics servicing motor-cars, but whereas we have appropriate criteria for judging the success or failure of the mechanic's tinkering, in the short run at least, how are we to tell what counts as success and failure in what goes on in school? Neither individual nor societal need-gratification can provide criteria, since all 'needs' themselves *presuppose* the value of the ends which they serve.

Finally, is there not something immoral, or perhaps amoral, in this entire business of manipulating individuals' tensions and living conditions for the sake of even the supposedly *best* of ends? Such treatment might be all right for animals, perhaps, and I doubt if there's a question of its being *morally* either 'right' or 'wrong' for either plants or machines; but is it right for children? Would it not imply a lack of respect for persons totally incompatible not only with what we feel to be moral but also with what we regard as of most value in education? And would it not be begging the question yet again to reply merely that children, as a matter of 'fact', are not 'really' persons *until* they have been educated, and that they do not merit or need treatment as persons, therefore, *while* they are being 'educated'?

2

Interests

1   Permissiveness and interests

Do children's 'interests' form any better basis for education than
individual and societal 'needs'?

The statement 'children learn through interest' is among the first
which a student is likely to hear in his college of education course.
But when he asks, naturally enough, what 'interest' is precisely, he
may find that no one seems altogether sure. A range of particular
examples may be pointed out to him. Children are 'interested' in
animals, in themselves, in teachers, in talking, in play; they are
often not interested, it appears, in mathematics, in history, in
writing, in work, and so on. But what 'interest' itself is, or what
sort of family of words it belongs to, remains elusive. Whereas
what is 'in one's interest' is usually expressed in terms of large,
adult, plausible, sorts of things such as a higher income, more
regular employment, better health and a longer life, the 'interests'
which children are said to 'learn through' seem to become more
minutely particularized, the closer one looks at them. The harder
one tries to fasten upon their lasting essence, the more fleeting they
grow. And of course, far from being adult and plausible, being the
interests of children they are often childish and absurd. In terms
of possible value, indeed, they may look a perfect rag-bag of the
trivial, the troublesome and the downright dangerous, bundled up
together. If this is the sort of medium through which children are
supposed to learn, one shudders to think what it is, at times, that
they could be learning. Children's 'interests', the student may now
conclude, are not always 'in their interest', and hardly ever 'in
others' interests' at all.

'Nevertheless,' he is told in his next lecture, perhaps, 'children
learn through interest.' The solution, then, is plain. Children must

be 'made' interested in what is in their and others' interests, so that they will learn it—after which all will be well. Teacher training, then, will be just a matter of teaching students some psychologically effective methods of 'making children interested' in what is (by general agreement) in everybody's interest. As K. M. Evans writes:

> Just as we can arrange for our children to acquire particular information and to learn particular skills, so we can arrange for them to acquire particular attitudes and interests. The techniques needed are fairly well understood. (1965, p. 141)

For teachers, then, it is simply a matter of mastering these techniques. By arranging for children to become interested in acquiring the information and skills which are in their and others' interests, we can enable them to learn these things 'through interest'.

But why bother to get them interested? What is the special virtue, the student now may ask, in their learning all these good things 'through interest'? If we can 'arrange' for children to acquire desirable information, skills, attitudes *and interests*, why go to the trouble of arranging for them to become *interested* in acquiring them? Is there something about 'learning through interest' which not only explains one of the ways in which we can get children to learn, but which is *itself* 'in their interest' somehow? Are 'interests' not just a motivational aid to learning something otherwise dull, but also *themselves* the sorts of things which children ought to be occupied with and learning about in school? But then, in that case, what about those trivial, troublesome, and dangerous interests already mentioned? Surely children ought not to be occupied with *them*?

At this point, perhaps, the student will be referred to the monograph on the subject which Dewey wrote over fifty years ago, or to one of his other essays or chapters on it, such as chapter 10 of *Democracy and Education* (1913; 1916). Dewey's monograph was directed against those who could see no relevance in interest for education except in terms of its making school a more pleasant and comfortable place for everyone concerned, by increasing pupils' motivation and thereby facilitating teachers' control. In other words he was concerned to argue that children's interests should not be treated *just* as a motivational aid. His point was that children will not only learn *quickly* what they are interested in, and that they will learn it in an untroublesome and co-operative sort of way, but also that what they are interested in is what they will learn *best*. The presence of interest, he pointed out, maximizes the likelihood that the pupil, when what he is interested in proves difficult or problematic, will put forth and sustain not just his greatest but also his *best* possible effort to master its difficulties. Whether the interesting activity is obviously in his and others' interests, as in learning to read, or not so obviously so, as in learning to reach the tip of his nose with his tongue, the significance of his *interest* is the same in either case, namely, that it will call forth his 'best' efforts.

But, of course, this just takes the discussion straight back to where it began. What is the significance of the word 'best', in Dewey's argument? What is the *particular* 'virtue' of interest, in education?

Dewey's opponents were quick to reply that although interested pupils perhaps learn 'best' in the sense of most rapidly and vigorously, *what* they learn is nevertheless not always 'best' in the sense of being most 'in everybody's interest'. What about such childishly interesting activities, for example, as biting one's nails? Many children show great interest in activities such as this, and no doubt they learn 'best' *about such activities* when they are interested in them, taking great pains over them and making every possible effort to get them right. As an aggrieved five-year-old said to me recently, 'I just *can't* bite my nails properly. I keep trying, but I can't do it *right*.' When apparently there *is* no virtue in an activity, such as in biting one's nails, how can it make *sense* to say that children do it 'best' when they are interested? If there's no 'good' in it, how could it be done 'better' or 'best'.

And who in his senses would say that children should go to school in order to engage in interesting activities (however effortfully undertaken and however well executed eventually) such as hair-pulling, paper-flicking, ink-slinging, bullying, chair-banging, teacher-baiting ... and so on? Again, what about all the trivial sorts of things which children show occasional interest in, such as wiggling their ears, standing on one leg, making themselves go cross-eyed, poking blotting paper into ink bottles or sticks into cracks in floors ... ? And what about those stereotyped and boringly derivative occupations which seem to make up the whole impoverished gamut of some children's interests? : the apparently endless stream of battle pictures criss-crossed with never-fading tracer bullets and explosions labelled 'Boom!' and 'Pow!'; the continual chatter about football, television, pop records; the comic-reading and gum-chewing; the pushing and shoving and all the pointless, tedious, repetitive and often blindly stupid or unkind things which children do, apparently, with great interest? Is this what they should go to school for, just to go on doing these 'with interest'? I remember vividly a boy who, on his first visit to the swimming baths with the class, ran straight up to the deep end, jumped in, and sank solidly to the bottom. He was chock-full of interest, and as a result of 'following' it he very nearly drowned. Was this 'education', on Dewey's view?

If teachers, believing themselves to be 'progressive', 'following Dewey', and so on, ever acted *consistently* on such an interpretation of Dewey as this, most of the children in their classes, and probably the teachers themselves too, would be dead or at least very badly damaged before the end of their first half term. In practice, students who start out with this view (and there are many) sensibly abandon it as soon as they are in a position to do so. An indiscriminately interest-gratifying view of schooling is plainly just as silly as an indiscriminately needs-gratifying one. It is no more educative to pander to every inclination which children have, than it is to satisfy every one of their demands on sight. But what, then, did Dewey mean? How could it be in the child's *educational* interest for him to 'learn through interest'? How could interest be *more* than a sometimes dangerous—and in any case rather 'soft'—motivational aid?

In the three sections of this chapter which follow, I shall consider in turn three of the several philosophical problems raised by Dewey's apparently straightforward slogan. First, 'learning through interest' requires at the very least that we be able to identify, recognize or diagnose what interests a child actually *has*. How can this be done? What does it *mean* to attempt such a task? Second, having analysed what would be involved in *locating* a child's interests, how could these be fostered or developed? Also, in what sense if any would it be possible to start him off on a totally 'new' interest? In other words, how could children's interests be aroused, or possibly 'made', and sustained? Third, what are we to think about the interests which children undoubtedly have in trivial, harmful or antisocial activities? In what sense if any are children learning 'best' when they are learning 'through' *these*? For that matter, in following *any* interest, what is it of specifically *educational* value which children are supposed to be learning thereby and which they could not learn as well in any other way?

These it seems to me are some, at least, of the problems which Dewey's writings on interest raise. Without some attempt to think clearly and carefully about them, one's educational theory—where it has any connection at all with what in practice one actually *does*—will remain caught in that ideological featherbedding of permissiveness which, as Cremin and other historians have argued (Cremin, 1964; Hofstadter, 1962), has been the bane of education for the last fifty years.

2 Identifying children's interests

First, then, how do we *know* a 'feeling of interest' when we 'feel' it? And how are we to *recognize* the existence of such feelings in others, and particularly in children?

These are logical questions, not psychological ones—which is just as well, since, after various pre-scientific writings earlier in this century (e.g. Adams, n.d.; McMurray, 1924), psychologists have had virtually nothing to say about interests, at least until very recently. Dominated as it has been by the 'needs and drives' model of action, the bulk of the psychological work at least of which I am aware has either contained no reference to 'interests' at all, or has quickly reduced the notion of 'interest' to the logical status of 'felt need'. Fairly permanent and settled sorts of interests thus become in this language 'need systems'. Actually occurring *feelings* of interest become for example 'activated "need pushes"' (McClelland, 1951, p. 595; Tolman, 1952, p. 69). But this strange jargon does nothing to clarify the nature of 'feelings of interest', nor to help us to *recognize* them either in ourselves or in others.

Just how empty of scientific practical guidance such an approach to 'interests' is, may be seen in the work of a writer such as Woodworth. For instance, writes Woodworth:

> The drive to actualize one's capacities would accordingly be an important source of a great variety of human interests. (1958, p. 140)

But if, say, I am interested in fishing, is the *source* of my interest a 'drive to actualize my capacities'? How could one possibly get hold of any concrete *evidence* for such a claim? If a child is interested in pulling the wings off flies, does this interest, too, have its 'source' in his 'drive to actualize his capacities'? How could we tell which interests derived from this 'source' and which from some other? And what experiments could we conceivably devise which might show that the drive was the 'source' of the interests, rather than the interests the 'source' of the drive? Above all, how would it help us in school to know that any child showing an interest in anything was doing so because he was being 'driven' to 'actualize his capacities'? Would this help either to *explain* why he was doing it, or to *justify* us in helping him to do it? Everyone has capacities (e.g. for being cruel) which it would be quite wrong to 'actualize', and the 'source' of whose interest (when they have any) itself needs explaining.

The logical character of interests is something which must be clarified before, not after, conducting psychological research into them. To assume as Woodworth and others do, that 'interests' stem *from* 'drives' and 'needs' is to prejudge issues of a scientific as well as of a logical kind. There is no evidence, of a scientific sort, which could show that I am only interested in fishing, for example, because I 'need' to be. And, on the face of it, in ordinary discourse we do not use the words 'need' and 'interest' in this way at all. We would be far more inclined to say that *if* I am interested in going fishing, *then* I will 'need' to do various other things such as getting bait, checking my gear, setting the alarm clock for an early hour, and so on. It would sound distinctly odd to say that under any circumstances I would ever 'need' to be interested in going fishing.

In this section, then, I shall be concerned, first, with questions about the logical categorization of feelings of interest, both in respect to the sort of 'feelings' which they are and to the sort of notion which 'interest' itself is, and, second, with questions about any special problems which may arise in connection with identifying and recognizing such feelings as these in ourselves and in others.

(a) *'Feelings of interest'* The philosophical analysis of concepts such as 'interest', 'attention', 'care', 'noticing', has been undertaken in a thoroughgoing way by A. R. White (1964; 1967), and it is upon his work that I must in the main depend.

To begin with, 'interest', in the sense in which I am concerned with it here, is not the sort of thing which we usually mean when we speak of someone as owning or acquiring an 'interest', say, in a business enterprise. To 'have an interest' in the Midland Bank, for example, normally means to own shares or something of the sort in

it, or in some way to have one's economic future intimately connected with *its* future. This is the sense of 'interest', too, in which
we speak of someone's hiring a lawyer or an accountant to protect
or look after his 'interests', and this is *not* the sense in which we
talk of children's 'interests' as being something which they 'learn
through'. By the 'interests' which children 'learn through' we mean
the things which they actually find interesting or 'feel interested'
in. Plainly one could own 'an interest' in a factory manufacturing,
say, drawing pins, yet not *find* the faintest interest nor *feel* the
slightest bit interested in its activities. As White says, 'An interested
party may be a bored one' (1964, p. 104).

'Interests', then, in the sense in which we are concerned with
them here, are not a sort of asset or liability which one can get hold
of or lose like a piece of property. They are a kind of inclination or
disposition. Specifically, as White puts it, 'interest' is:

> ... an inclination to engage in some one or more perceptual,
> intellectual, or practical activities that are appropriate to the
> particular object of interest. (1967, p. 85)

or, as he puts it in his earlier book:

> To feel interested in anything is to feel attracted to it; to *feel
> inclined* to give attention to it. Naturally, it also involves feeling
> disinclined to attend to other things, and feeling vexed, unhappy
> and uncomfortable, when prevented from giving attention to it.
> (1964, p. 104)

Actually *feeling* inclined in this way is what White calls having
an 'occurrent' interest, but of course we may also *be* so inclined
without *feeling* that way here and now. For example, I may be
interested in the music of Bach, without actually feeling at this
very moment inclined to put down my pen and switch on the
record-player. 'Being interested' in this sense is what White calls
having a 'dispositional' as opposed to an 'occurrent' interest (op.
cit., p. 102).

'Children's interests', then, are the fairly settled *dispositions*
which they have to notice, to pay attention to, and to engage in
some appropriate activity with certain sorts of things rather than
others—as evidenced from time to time by their occurrent *inclinations* to behave in these ways. An 'interested' child, therefore, is one
who is characteristically active, attentive and absorbed in ways
appropriate to his interest—and it is particularly important at this

point to notice that the word 'appropriate' here refers to his *interest*, and not necessarily to anybody's view of what might be 'appropriate' to *him* or of what might be appropriate to the possibly insignificant-looking thing which he seems to be interested *in*. Most small boys, for example, will say that they are interested in 'football', but they may be able to play it just as well (or in ways just as 'appropriate to their interest') with an old beachball or a tennis ball or perhaps anything at all which will roll about fairly freely when kicked, as with a 'real' football such as you or I might feel appropriate to *our* interest in the game.

The importance of this point will come out more clearly in section 3, below, when we come to consider what is meant by trying to 'sustain' children's interests. At the present stage in the discussion, however, it should be clear that what we mean by an interest in 'football', for example, must be an inclination towards attentive activity in a *flexible* range of matters, some of which might be perhaps only very loosely connected with what you or I might understand as the game. To insist that the boys play to the strict rules of *our* version of the game, with a 'proper' ball and so on, may be the very thing which they are *not* 'interested' in. Similarly, to insist that being interested in football is something 'appropriate' for small boys but not, for example, for small girls, may again do violence to the actual 'feeling of interest' which a particular child, boy or girl, is feeling. An interest may sometimes seem wildly 'inappropriate' both to the person who shows it and to any conventional views as to its nature, and yet be a perfectly genuine interest for all that.

What the child's interest is will depend on what it is that he notices or goes on attending to, and what it suggests to him in the way of 'appropriate activity'. Any label, such as 'football', 'stamp-collecting', 'fishing', which we give or which he gives to his interest will designate no more than a fraction of what the interest actually *is*, and any particular label may sometimes prove more misleading than helpful as a way of identifying the interest. His interest is what the child *feels* from time to time inclined to do attentively, and thus to find out more about. What he finds interesting, he does for *its* interest—not because he needs to do it on any *other* account or for any *other* reason. One mistake, then, which we may make about the identification of children's interests is to assume that they are necessarily going to be some sort of approximation to adult interests, or that they must necessarily have some 'normal' range of content at any particular age or stage in a culture. Statistics could never 'prove' that certain interests were 'normal' and others not, since the correct compiling of the statistics would itself be dependent upon some *non*-statistical way of correctly identifying those interests. Most small boys may *say* that they are interested in football, but what they *are* interested in, or what they *mean* by 'football', is something which will vary in each individual case.

A second kind of mistake in identification may arise over the kind of 'feeling' which we may assume that children's interests contain. Here again White's work is particularly helpful. He compares 'feelings of interest', first, with what he calls 'sensory and perceptual feelings':

> 'Feeling' interested is obviously not a perceptual feeling like feeling a hole in my pocket nor is it an exploration like feeling for a light switch. Neither is someone who is interested in what he is doing necessarily having any sensations, faint or acute, steady or intermittent, localisable or general. Such sensations would distract him from the object of his interest. (op. cit., p. 104)

Merely to plunge children into a range of sensory and perceptual 'feelings' or in other words to 'give them experiences', then, as teachers might do when they are trying to 'stimulate creative writing', for example, is as likely to distract children *from* their interests as to forward them. Of course, children might by chance *find* such 'feelings' interesting, but on the face of it even this would seem more likely to happen if the 'feelings' were encountered actually in the course of pursuing some interest. When 'feeling' his way along the branch of a tree, for example, or 'feeling' for sweets at the back of the cupboard, or again when 'feeling' the sorts of sensations which are part of interesting activities such as swimming or playing flickers—in cases such as these, a child might get to 'feel interested', I suppose, in the sensory and perceptual 'feelings' themselves. Usually, however, an interest purely *in* such 'feelings', in abstraction from any interesting pursuit of which they formed a part, is something which we would expect to find in a person of rather exceptional and specialized training, such as a neurologist or a phenomenological psychologist. And in any case, the 'sensory and perceptual feelings' would not be the same *as* the 'feeling of interest'.

Secondly, White points out, 'feelings' of interest may be confused with moods and emotions. To begin with:

> An interest is not a mood, like cheerfulness or gloominess; it has a definite object. (1967, p. 83)

To claim to be interested, without being able to point out what it is that one is interested *in*, would be nonsensical. By contrast, a characteristic thing about moods such as depression, for example, is their pervasiveness, their lack of an identifiable focus. If one 'feels' depressed, *everything* is depressing. If one 'feels' interested, one 'feels' it about something in particular. The sort of mood-setting, then, such as playing gramophone records or covering a corner of the classroom with different shades of blue, which may go on when teachers nowadays are trying to 'spark off interest', is often entirely misconceived. Some moods, it is true, may be a *precondition* of the arousal of interest—confidence, for example. But just aiming at setting up a mood-state is not the same *as* starting off an interest. Without some illuminating guidance as to the *sort* of interest which their teacher has in mind in 'the blue corner' or when putting on the record of *Fingal's Cave*, children may pass through a succession of moods (e.g. apprehension, anxiety, bewilderment, boredom) but are certainly not 'being interested'.

Emotions have more precise objects than moods do, and in this at least are a little more akin to 'feelings of interest' than are mood-states. Again, however, being in an emotional state is, as White points out, quite different from being interested. In particular, 'feelings of interest' lack the excited or 'stirred-up' quality which one finds in emotions such as fear, anger, joy and so on. One can be afraid, for example, too, without necessarily being interested in whatever it is that one is afraid of (e.g. an electrical storm), just as one can be interested (e.g. in electrical storms) without necessarily feeling emotional about the interesting object in any way at all. Indeed, an overpowering emotion may block a developing interest, just as the discovery of a new interest in something may lead to the experience of different emotions in its presence. Thus, as White says:

> Feeling interested is ... not an emotional or stirred-up state, such as feeling excited or thrilled, agitated or surprised. You cannot be 'beside yourself' or 'speechless' with interest; nor does increasing interest disturb your concentration, as mounting excitement or anxiety may. (ibid.)

Emotions, then, like moods, are only circumstantially, not logically, connected with 'feelings of interest'.

This is particularly important, I think, in connection with a 'stirred-up state' such as excitement, for here again, because of the confusion of such states with 'feelings of interest', one may find teachers perhaps trying to *interest* children by using methods which in fact constitute the very thing most likely to *prevent* an interest (at least for the time being) from developing. Characteristically one may be 'excited' by the *prospect* of doing something interesting. While one waits to be able to get on and do it, excitement mounts, but nothing *interesting* is happening. One's *interest* is neither being aroused nor being developed by the mounting *excitement*. Merely excited children, whose emotions have been agitated or 'stirred up' by some purportedly 'interesting' prospect which their teacher has conjured up, are typically very demanding, very dependent and in a highly unstable state which increasingly approaches the limit of their self-control. Teachers promising a class outing, a film, a game, or doing anything which is not *itself* interesting but merely an 'exciting' or 'stimulating' prelude to activities or events which the children are led to believe *will be* interesting, are putting their children into a sort of Christmas Eve situation whose outcome is as likely to be deflating as inspiring. They are not arousing 'feelings of interest', but merely stirring up emotions. What is 'sparked off', and what so soon fizzles out, is excitement, not interest. The mistake plainly lies in confusing an emotional state, or what White calls an 'agitation' (1967, p. 116), with a 'feeling of interest'.

Finally, pleasures and pains are of course 'feelings' of a kind, and these, too, may be confused with 'feelings of interest'. Both moods and emotions, on the one hand, and sensory or perceptual feelings, on the other hand, may be more or less pleasurable or painful in what psychologists call their 'feeling tone'. But the fact that some sensations are usually pleasant, or have maybe a sort of 'fun feeling' about them, is logically irrelevant to the question of whether or not they are interesting. An interest specifically *in* pleasant sensations or 'fun feeling' *as such* argues again a child of unusually specialized preoccupations—and again, the interest *in* pleasure or *in* fun, in any case, is not the same thing as the 'feeling' *of* pleasure or *of* fun. Similarly, pleasurable moods and emotions such as contentment, joy, confidence, satisfaction and so on, which White calls 'completions' (loc. cit.), have no *logical* connection with 'feelings of interest'. A child playing football may be joyful one moment, in despair the next, getting pleasure from making a good tackle, suffering agonies from a kick on the shins—and none of these fluctuating pleasures and pains will necessarily mean that he has a fluctuating *interest* in the game. His interest is not *logically* dependent upon his getting pleasure. Doing something 'for its interest' is entirely different from doing something with the idea of 'getting pleasure' or 'having fun', and here again teachers who confuse the two sorts of 'feeling' may be misled into thinking that by keeping their classes 'happy' or by giving their children 'pleasure' or 'fun' they are following Dewey's doctrine that children 'learn best through interest'. 'Through interest' one can as readily be led to pains as to pleasures, and to despair as to happiness. The outcome of one's interests in terms of pleasure, pain, joy, sorrow and so on, is entirely contingent upon what one is interested *in* and upon the degree of success which one sees oneself as achieving in one's efforts to do what seems apropriate *to* those interests. To say that a child who blows himself up on Guy Fawkes' night could not have been 'interested' in rockets, or to say that Schumann could not have been 'really' interested in playing the piano or Virginia Woolf in the art of the novel, merely because their efforts did not end in pleasure or happiness, would be absurd.

Interests, as we have seen, are inclinations—and for the most part, of course, people *are* 'inclined' to seek pleasure and avoid pain. However, there are many things which we are *inclined* to do, but which we are not necessarily *interested in doing*. Habits and impulses, for example, may show the kind of behaviour which one is regularly or irregularly 'inclined' or 'prone' to engage in under certain circumstances. I may fairly regularly feel inclined to smoke a pipe, for instance, or in other words I may have a pipe-smoking 'habit'. I may now and again experience an impulse, or irregularly 'feel inclined', to switch off the alarm-clock on a winter morning and go straight back to sleep. But I do not necessarily 'feel an interest' in what I am either habitually or impulsively inclined to do. Similarly, the objects of my likings and preferences, although they show some of the forms currently taken by my inclinations to seek pleasure and avoid pain, are not necessarily the same as the things which I currently find interesting. I may like plum jam, or prefer it to strawberry, without necessarily being in the slightest degree interested in either of them. The fact that if you offer me both, I'll be inclined to choose the former, will show you my preference but not necessarily indicate anything at all about my interests.

Children, of course, have innumerable likings and preferences, and are also especially prone to behaving impulsively and to forming rather rigid and stereotyped habits of action. None of these four forms of 'inclination', however, is logically in the same category as the inclination to notice, to pay attention to, and to engage in action appropriate to one's interests. The connection of children's likes, preferences, impulses and habits, therefore, with their interests, where it exists at all is probably entirely fortuitous. Letting children just do as they like or prefer, or as impulse or habit inclines them, is therefore not the same thing at all as letting them 'pursue their interests'. What they are interested in, they are inclined to pursue —for this, as we have seen, is partly what 'feeling interested' *means*. But not everything which they are *inclined* to do will be pursued by them for its *interest*. It might just as easily be pursued for its pleasure or from liking or preference, or merely out of impulse or habit.

So much, then, for the *sort* of thing, very roughly, which we are looking for, when we are trying to discover children's 'interests'. I have skimmed over the surface of many philosophical issues here which readers may care to follow up further. White's work itself, for example, of which I have touched on only a fraction, is closely linked with that of Ryle (1949), especially in connection with the topic of 'dispositions' and 'inclinations' and with the classification of 'interest' as a notion within this category. As to 'likings' and 'preferences', some particularly helpful articles on these have appeared recently by writers such as Pashman (1968), Leiber (1968) and Rachels (1969), and references to these should be made also in connection with the topic of 'reasons for action' which is discussed in section 4a below. A more general contemporary review of the subject of 'pleasures and pains' can be found in Cowan (1968).

(b) *'Showing an interest'* I turn now to the second of the two problems involved in identifying children's interests. The first is to know what sort of thing we are looking for; and this, or at least some features of this, I have tried to indicate in (a) above: a 'feeling of interest' is not a set of sensations, nor a mood or emotion, nor an inclination to get or repeat pleasure, nor an impulse or habit. It is by contrast an inclination to notice something, to pay continuing attention to it and to try to enter into some active relationship with it which seems appropriate to its interesting features. Second, however, we must now ask whether there are any special difficulties involved in *recognizing* the sort of thing which we now know that we are looking for—for this too, worse luck, is not as simple a task as it might seem.

We might, for example, be tempted to say: 'I want my children to "learn through interest". Well, then, I'll simply ask them what their interests are, as a first step. After that, I'll collect together the resources relevant to those interests—and then they'll be able to get on with it!' Unfortunately, however, children can never just *say* what their interests are. Merely because they, not we, *feel* their 'feelings of interest', it does not in the least follow that they will *know* best what those feelings are. For the interpretation of their feelings ('of interest', as of anything else) they have to rely on empirical clues and features which are as visible to us as to them. There is no specific quality of feeling which comes into experience ready-labelled, as it were, with 'This is a feeling of interest', 'This is a feeling of envy', 'This is anxiety', 'This is enjoyment', like an identification-tag tied to it. Like us, children need more than just to *feel* their feelings, before they can communicate to others what their feelings *are*.

Of course, it is true that all feelings, thoughts and indeed 'experiences' in general, are in a sense 'private' to the person who has them. (For an exceptionally clear discussion of this controversial sort of 'privacy', see Cowan, op. cit., especially pp. 48-9.) But it does not follow that because I am the only person who can (logically speaking) 'feel' *my* feelings or 'think' *my* thoughts, therefore no one else can *know* as well as I do (or better) what their significance may be. It is certainly a fundamental error of theory, then, to suppose that children can simply *tell* their teachers what their interests are. More probably, if asked what they are interested in, they won't even understand the question.

Can teachers, in that case, just look and *see* whether or not a child is interested in what he is doing or proposes doing? In a sense, yes; but only in a vastly oversimplified sense. Children can 'show' an interest, even if they cannot communicate it verbally or by the sorts of gestures or expressions such as 'Ouch!' and 'Ah!' which 'show' pleasure or pain. But even the interpretation of expressions of pleasure and pain can raise difficulties. 'Does that hurt?' asks the doctor, while we wince, flinch, cry 'Ouch!' and 'show' clearly (one would imagine) that it *does*. He seems to require some *verbal* confirmation of what our behaviour 'shows'. Where such verbal endorsements are impossible, as with a very small baby, judgment can be extremely tricky indeed. All parents, for example, know the difficulty of deciding whether baby's cries in the middle of the night mean hunger, wind, or for instance just a wish to be picked up and played with. But even where the aid of words *is* available (and this is something which itself will vary from child to child), judgments have still to be made as to their truth and accuracy. An interest, like a pleasure or a pain, can be as readily 'concealed' or 'feigned' as it can be 'shown'.

If mistakes can be made about something so straightforward, seemingly, as whether or not one is in pain, it should be plain that recognizing whether or not a child is 'showing an interest' will never be a simple matter. Not only is he usually unable (and often unwilling) to give us reliable *verbal* guidance, the experience of 'being interested' is itself so much more complex than the experience, say, of pain or pleasure, that difficulties are bound to arise. In its level of complexity, 'being interested' is more like being in love than being pleased.

More than a difference in the level of complexity, however, is also involved. Just *observing* a child no more readily enables us to diagnose his interests than merely *observing* the activities, for example, of a magistrate enables us to 'see' or 'hear' the justice or wisdom of his pronouncements. There is no particular event or activity which 'shows' the judge's wisdom. Similarly, in a sense there is no particular happening or circumstance which we could take as a sufficient condition of someone's 'being interested'. If a persons hits his thumb with a hammer or drops a brick on his toe, usually we can say with at least some certainty, 'That *must* have hurt!' but there are no comparable circumstances in which we can say of a situation 'That *must* be interesting!' Further, when the person who hit his thumb then throws the hammer down and hops around swearing, shouting 'Ouch!' and so on, we can fairly reliably in most cases take this as confirmation that the blow did 'really' hurt, but there is no *particular* behaviour which confirms to the same degree that someone 'really' is interested. Similarly there is no particular behaviour sufficient to 'show' that a person is in love (rather, say, than infatuated), or that he is engaged in delivering pronouncements which are wise and just.

The behavioural criteria of 'being interested' are implicit in the logical features of the notion of 'interest' itself. They include, therefore, such things as noticing, paying attention, persisting in one's efforts in an absorbed or undistracted way. None of these kinds of behaviour, however, are *sufficient* to 'show' interest for sure. The problem, from our point of view, is that there is no *further* sort of behaviour or event which conceivably *could* 'show' it in any other *kind* of way. As White says:

> ... concealing your interest does not mean keeping any activities hidden in the way that concealing the fact that you are attending does. Nor does it mean that you keep any results to yourself, as must the man who tries to pretend that he has not noticed anything. (op. cit., p. 106)

Similarly, 'showing' your interest does not mean revealing or displaying any particular and unmistakable sort of sign by which your interest must certainly be detected. Children do not 'show' their interests as a leopard shows his spots, or as a sufferer shows his pain, or even as an attentive listener shows his attention. Exactly the same observable circumstances may be interesting to one child, tedious to another. And exactly the same observable behaviour may be engaged in by a child who is interested, side by side with a child who is bored. Nor is there any 'internal' or 'private' and 'unobservable' kind of 'behaviour' going on in one child but not in the other, which, if disclosed or discovered, would provide an infallible mode of distinguishing between the two.

However, noticing, attending and persisting in appropriate effort, though not sufficient signs of the presence of interest, are at least *necessary* ones—and I doubt if we should expect more help than this. The truth, of course, is that 'interest', like 'love', 'justice' and 'wisdom', is not just an empirical but also an evaluative notion. No observable features, by themselves, are sufficient to make something interesting, any more than to make it lovable, just or wise, and no particular psychic kick, thrill, tingle or anything else, nor any gesture or posture or piece of behaviour expressive of such psychic events, *in itself* corresponds to what we mean by 'feeling' and 'showing' interest. 'Finding an interest' means becoming inclined to think something in itself *worth* notice, attention and an effort to find ways of relating to it in an *appropriate* manner. Neither its worth, nor what is appropriate to it, are matters simply for observation.

I shall return to the connection between interests and values in

4(a), below. For the present I am concerned to stress that certain theoretical assumptions which in my experience are widespread—that children's interests are plain to see, that all children have much the same interests anyway (at appropriate ages and stages), and that if there is any doubt about a particular child's interests we need merely to instruct him to consult his 'feelings' and report back upon what he finds—must be entirely false. To say that the child knows best what interests him, or that the teacher, the parent, the developmental psychologist or anyone else knows best, is just not true. It is also extremely misleading. To send students on teaching practice, for example, in conditions which make it quite impossible for them to get to know their children properly, and at the same time to lead those students to believe that a good teacher is one who 'considers children's interests', puts both students and children in an impossible situation. Implicit in a child's interests is all that is most personal and unique about him. To claim to have discovered this after a few weeks in a crowded classroom is absurd. In practice, of course, most students quickly and sensibly abandon the attempt—and, with it, most of their 'theory'. Where the claim still continues to be made, however, that in such situations learning is being 'based on children's interests', I can only think that those who make it are doing no more than indulge in some vague ideological gesture.

A child's behaviour may mask his interests as readily as it reveals them. He may feign interest in order to please us, conceal interest in order to deceive us, and of course he is as likely to try to please and to deceive *himself*, at times, as to do so to others. If children have no confidence, either in others or in themselves, then to show an unfeigned interest will seem to them like courting disaster. Even in circumstances of mutual respect and trust, however, interests, like anything else which we can 'see' or be 'shown', require interpretation. By themselves the *logical* difficulties implicit, as Wittgenstein has shown (1953; 1958), in the very *notions* of 'identification' and 'recognition' should caution us against diagnosing people's interests in a facile way, even if the *psychological* difficulties of the task apparently do not.

3 Originating, arousing and sustaining interest

For many teachers, as I explained in section 6 of chapter 1, interest is nothing more than a motivational aid, or in other words a means of inducing children to undertake tasks which to the children themselves are tedious but which, from the teacher's point of view, represent some desirable goal or norm of schooling. Personally, as I shall argue further in 4(b) below, I can see nothing *educative* in this at all, though it may be an efficient enough way of getting children 'schooled', in certain circumstances—and a more pleasant method, of course, than just applying a stick to their bottoms. What is disturbing, however, from the point of view of an interest-based rather than a needs-based philosophy of education, is to hear it alleged that by hooking children's interests to tedious tasks, so that they will have to get the tasks done before they can return to the pursuit of their interests, the teacher is 'making' the tasks interesting or 'making' the children interested in the tasks.

Nothing could be further from the truth. Such a teacher is not 'making' anything interesting at all. On the one hand he is trivializing children's interests, by treating them merely as means to ends. On the other hand he is devaluing the tasks themselves, by implicitly admitting to the children that they are the sorts of tasks which in fact any sensible person would only undertake for a fee. It is this sort of teacher-strategy which Dewey plainly had in mind in the following passage:

> When things have to be *made* interesting, it is because interest itself is wanting. Moreover, the phrase is a misnomer. The thing, the object, is no more interesting than it was before. The appeal is simply made to the child's love of something else. (1913, pp. 11-12)

One can *make use of* a child's interest in X (e.g. in pleasing his parents) in order to get him to perform an instructional task Y (e.g. working at his O levels), but this is not 'making him interested' in Y nor 'making Y interesting' to him. It is not originating in him an inclination to try to undertake behaviour appropriate to Y for its own sake. Indeed the question of what Y is worth *for its own sake* does not even arise. The worth of Y from the start is presented as deriving solely from its being a means of securing X. The *interest* of Y is nil, and the only sense in which the child 'learns Y' is that he submits to performing the tasks designated by the teacher *as* 'learning Y'. He learns nothing of its interest, for, in the way in which it is being presented, it has none.

The psychologists Sears and Hilgard, in a well-known essay on motivational aids to learning, express clearly this reduction of learning to performance which is implied in the strategy of treating interest as a motivational aid and of which I have already given some account in sections 4 and 6 of chapter 1. When children are put in a situation in which they *need* to learn Y in order to promote their *interest* in X, then 'learning Y' becomes increasingly a matter merely of carrying on a performance of the required kind. Thus, say Sears and Hilgard:

> For purposes, such as those of instruction, the distinction between learning and performance becomes somewhat less important, since what keeps the pupil performing is also likely to keep him learning. (1964, p. 182)

Because the teacher has the situation firmly in control, through his strategy of controlling the child's access to what he finds interesting (X), the pupil has to keep performing Y—and 'performing Y' will mean keeping busy on any set of tasks which *to the teacher* equate with 'desirable learning'.

There are innumerable ways in which this can work out in practice. The connection between X and Y need not be *completely* arbitrary and contingent, as in the examples of 'pleasing one's parents' and 'working at one's O levels' which I mentioned just now. Often, in primary schools especially, pupils may be 'kept performing' (for a while, anyway) by a deployment of tasks (Y) at least *superficially* connected with the interest (X) and therefore at least holding out some *promise* of being interesting.

For example, if the child expresses an interest in something to do with aeroplanes, flying, getting about fast, things that go 'Zoom!', and so on, he may find himself rapidly deployed into the production of an 'interest book', labelled, say, 'The History Of Aeroplanes', or even, 'Transport Through The Ages'. The book has to be fairly neat and tidy of course (to constitute a 'book'), and to involve writing, and copying bits out of other books, and 'doing pictures', and cutting out and pasting in—all adding up to an overall performance which the *teacher* sees as constituting 'desirable learning'. 'Performing' Y becomes 'learning' through Y, or at any rate the distinction between them 'becomes somewhat less important'—less important, that is (in a classroom where anything from thirty to fifty children at once must somehow be kept 'desirably learning'), than the sheer mechanics of keeping the performance going.

Meanwhile the child's initial interest (X), about which the teacher knows no more at the end than he did at the beginning, remains unexplored and undeveloped. It might have had more to do with the idea of witches flying about on broomsticks than with 'The History Of Aeroplanes', and, at least on the face of it, it had no more than a superficial connection with an activity in which the necessary work involved principally writing, copying, drawing, and making a 'book'. If the child can be 'kept performing', he learns *about* the performance, not about his interest. Whatever else he learns, he learns through the *performance*, not 'through interest'. He learns, indeed, simply to carry on the performance of 'making an interest book', but he learns nothing more of his interest. His interest, therefore, remains at its initial conceptual level of more or less childish fantasy, and his ability to 'learn' becomes increasingly a matter of being able to persist in the performance of tasks of a more or less mechanical kind. Certainly, through the teacher's strategy of using interest as a motivational aid, the child is not 'made interested' in anything, and nothing new is 'made interesting' to him.

For a long time, in reaction I suppose against manipulative strategies such as these, I was unwilling personally to admit that interests *could* be engendered or deliberately started off, by teachers or by anyone else. Although, for reasons which I shall give shortly, I no longer think this, I remain convinced that the more or less arbitrary connection of pre-selected subject-matter with children's existing interests is more likely to kill the existing interests than to create new ones. Sometimes, no doubt, a new interest *does* appear during the course of this treatment, in the same sort of way that occasionally a child *may* acquire a taste for his medicine after being many times induced to swallow it by the offer of a sweet. But, even if a pupil does eventually grow interested in a subject originally studied for the sake of an entirely different interest, no credit for this can lie with a teacher whose only reason for 'stimulating interests' was in order to make use of them as motivational aids. Such a teacher has not even been *trying* to get the child interested in the subject, but merely to engage repeatedly in the performance of 'taking' it.

To try deliberately to bring a new interest into being, therefore, has nothing in common with using psychological pressures to induce children to undertake performances. As White says:

Interest is not explicable by attention. Nor can it be explained in terms of motives or reasons. Being or becoming interested, or showing an interest, is not something we intentionally do, it is something we cannot here and now help. To explain a continuing interest is to discover the source of a proneness. (op. cit., p. 109)

Nothing which merely sets out to obligate, or tempt, or make children want or wish to become interested, can 'make' them do so. It would be like trying to *make* them prefer plum jam to strawberry. We could make them *select* it; we could not make them *like* it. Similarly, we can make children pay attention to their sums and *try* to do all the things which they believe will enable them to get them right. But we cannot in the same way make them *interested* in getting them right.

In White's later book he puts the point this way:

Attention may be demanded; interest has to be aroused ... It is unfair to blame someone for not showing an interest ... Trying to get interested in something is somewhat like trying to feel sorry for someone; neither is a matter of trying to *do*. (1967, p. 84)

We cannot get children interested in something by getting them to *do* anything. We have to *teach* them the interest of it. Its interest is something to be *learned*, in a sense quite different from that in which 'learning' is 'performing', and more like that in which it means 'seeing the point' or 'getting to understand'. Getting to understand what logically speaking *makes* a sum 'right' is quite different from just trying to *get* the sum right. Getting to understand what makes a person's state a 'sorry' one, is different from just getting into a sorrowful frame of mind about him. 'Getting to understand', like 'becoming inclined', is not a matter in White's phrase of 'trying to *do*', nor a matter of being 'made' psychologically to do, anything at all. You cannot *make* me acquire a taste for stout and oysters, or an interest in Shakespeare or cricket, but you can try to *teach* me the distinctive point of these things. If you try to *make* me see the point of them, I'm liable to start wondering what your motives are, and to question whether you are genuinely interested in them yourself.

At the beginning of section 2 above, I mentioned the dearth of psychological research on interests and the tendency of psychologists generally speaking to class 'interest' as some sort of 'need'. Over the last decade or so, however, and largely as a result of the detailed studies of children by Piaget (e.g. 1953; 1955), some psychologists have begun to look again at the topic of what they call 'intrinsic motivation', or in other words interest. One of the best accounts of this work, as far as it has gone, is contained in chapters 3 and 4 of J. McV. Hunt's *The Challenge of Incompetence and Poverty* (1969). Chapter 3 is very largely a review of the inadequacies of the conventional 'needs and drives' account of motivation. Towards the end, however, and throughout chapter 4 Hunt puts forward a version of the way in which interests are first formed and of their early changes in form ('The epigenesis of intrinsic motivation', as he calls it) which might do much to help us, in White's phrase, 'to discover the source of a proneness'. At this point, therefore, I must interrupt my attempt to see what may be involved *philosophically* in the genesis or origination of interests, in order to take account of what Hunt claims to have discovered empirically about the matter.

An interest, Hunt says, passes through three necessary stages in its formation. First, some sort of orienting response to something in the environment (or, as he puts it, to an optimum variation in sensory input) is essential. In other words, if we noticed nothing we would not become interested in anything. Second, he says, after repeated encounters with the noticed object or whatever it is, there begins to develop an 'emotional attachment deriving from cognitive familiarity' (op. cit., p. 89). Thus, in his words:

> The avidity of an infant's interest in the world may seem to be in large part a function of the variety of situations he has encountered repeatedly, (p. 101)

Third, the now-established interest is kept alive by the occurrence of continuing novelties or incongruities within the familiar situation. Too much incongruity or 'dissonance' (see Festinger, 1957) produces fear, too little produces boredom. To sustain interest there must be a sort of optimum discrepancy, the calculating of which Hunt calls the 'problem of the match'. The three stages, then, are:

> ... 'orienting response' to stimulus change, recognition with repeated encounters, and interest in the variations within the familiar. (p. 104)

These three, together, constitute the 'epigenesis of intrinsic motivation'.

Now I think that all this, after we have fought our way through the jargon, sounds very hopeful and promising for teachers and might at last begin to provide them with some practical psychological guidance regarding 'learning through interest'. But, as it stands, it is still not a *logically* complete account of how interests are engendered and sustained. It does not explain why *some* environmental or 'stimulus' changes can produce an 'orienting response' while others do not, nor (second) why the repetition of 'stimuli' which on the first occasion were noteworthy are not on *all* subsequent occasions disregarded, nor (third) why 'variations within the familiar' are not always, for example, irritating or bewildering rather than sometimes interesting.

To put this in another way: if Hunt's account were fundamentally correct as it stands, then once again (as in the 'needs and drives' account) we should have to believe that it was possible to do exactly the thing which I have argued above, and which White has argued, it would never logically speaking be possible to do— namely, to 'make' children interested by manipulating their environment and behaviour. We should merely have to set up the sort of environmental stimulation which *makes* them 'orient', and then repeat this with variations calculatedly 'matched' to their individual cognitive levels. But 'interest' is not just an 'emotional attachment' to the familiar. Perhaps indeed, as I have argued, it is not fundamentally an *emotional* sort of thing at all, but, even if 'interest' *were* an emotion, it would be a mistake to identify it *just* with the sorts of emotion which familiarity may arouse. Familiarity, for example, may be reassuring, comforting, boring, sickening, contemptible ... and so on. Only when the 'variations' within it can be seen to have some intrinsic *point*, are they liable to seem interesting and is the familiarity itself a matter of any interest. An *interestingly* varying situation is more like a set of musical variations upon a theme, than like the product of a set of psychometric calculations.

Similarly, to respond ('orient') *with interest* is not the same thing as noticing something or giving it your attention. The very example which Hunt gives as illustration of an 'orienting response'—namely, noticing the clock in the room when it suddenly stops ticking— is exactly the same one which White gives to illustrate, not the dawning of one's *interest*, but the drawing of one's *attention*. As White puts it:

> ... what draws my attention to the clock is its suddenly ceasing to tick or its going off with a bang. (1964, p. 109)

By following Hunt's directions we might be able to make children *attend* (momentarily, anyway)—and many teachers in fact do this already by setting up, for example, what is called 'a stimulating environment'—but, even if the children got 'emotionally attached' to having this sort of environment around, we would still not be 'making them interested' in it. To quote White again:

> Attention ... cannot explain the doing of anything nor an inclination to do anything. We may attend because we are interested, we are not interested because we attend. (loc. cit.)

Most infants display 'orienting responses' to things which go off with a bang, but, even when they get 'emotionally attached' to them, I can see no reason for calling this stage one and stage two of the epigenesis of *interest*. 'Orienting responses' are as often the *results* of interest, I would guess, as the sources of it. Intriguing or making children curious, seem to me at least as often *parasitic upon* their existing interests, rather than ways of generating new ones.

I return, then, to the point which I had reached before this psychological digression, namely that, so far as I can see, the only way of engendering interest in anything is through helping the child to see something of its significance. 'Stimulating' behaviour by teachers in classrooms (e.g. blowing soap bubbles across the room, setting fire to newspapers, starting a 'blue corner' or an 'interest table', playing electronic sound-effects records) may 'make' children excited, astonished, apprehensive, bewildered, indifferent, and so on, but unless there *is* something of intelligible interest in what the teacher is doing nothing *of* interest is likely to develop. The most that a teacher can do, I think, is to try to communicate *his* view of what is interesting in an *intelligible* way. In a sense it must be interest itself which engenders and arouses interest, but it only does so if one can somehow *show* to others what it is that seems interesting. After that, whether or not they make an 'orienting response' to it, is not a determinable event.

Finally, in this section, we must notice that neither *arousing* a dispositional interest nor *engendering* an occurrent one is the same thing as 'sustaining' an interest once it exists. It is entirely catastrophic to the whole enterprise of 'learning through interest' to suggest that once children *are* interested there is nothing much for the teacher to do but stand back and let them get on with it. On this unfortunate theory, teachers should 'keep in the background' and just *allow* interests to be followed. We do not expect a child of two to be able to pursue his interests entirely without help. Why, then, should we think that a child of five, ten or fifteen, or for that matter an adult of fifty, whose interests by this time are correspondingly more complex, will be able to pursue them unaided?

There are ideological reasons for this assumption, which I shall have to make some reference to in section 4 and in later chapters below, for example in connection with the notion of 'child-centred education'. For the present it is the sheer impracticality of the idea which I want to stress. An interest is an inclination to pay attention to something and to enter into appropriate active relationships with it. A child, and often an adult, cannot simply *see* what to do in the furtherance of his interest, as though its cognitive and practical implications were somehow written on it like the instructions on a puncture outfit. He has to learn what these implications *may be*, and the function of teachers is to *help* him to do so, if they want him to 'learn through interest'. The point (on this view) of his going to school *is* that he should there be able to receive some expert help. It is entirely pointless, therefore, to send him off to school and then leave him there like a sort of cultural Robinson Crusoe, while teachers and others, like friendly passing ships, drop off a few stores now and then to sustain his intellectual and other 'basic needs'. Every child wishes that he *knew* how to do 'properly' what he is interested in doing—since the inclination to *try* to do just this is what 'being interested' *means*. For his interest to be sustained, then, he must make progress in *learning* how to pursue his interest and, in doing so, learn more of what is involved *in* that interest itself.

Along with expert help in learning, he needs some sort of enabling environment which contains resources to pursue his interests *with*. Without variety of content and flexibility of access in this respect, he might be better off at home or in the streets. Moreover the environment must of course be socially, as well as materially, helpful. How thirty to fifty children could ever *really* be expected to 'learn through interest' while kept in one room, for example, is beyond my imagination. Such a setting, for five hours a day, would impoverish the interests of *one* child, let alone of forty. Add to this a doctrine which stipulates in effect that the teacher has no responsibility for sustaining interest anyway, or that he is to do little more than stop fights and give out supplies, and one begins to understand why in practice so-called 'learning through interest' may become an aimless free-for-all in which children's interests grow increasingly trivial, destructive or strategically concealed.

4 *Undesirable interests*

Not only is leaving children to their own devices unlikely to help them to sustain and develop their interests. It raises other problems too, as the following passage from the Plowden Report may serve to illustrate:

> A group of H.M.I.s working in a division in which some particularly good work is to be found, write as follows:— 'The newer methods start with the direct impact of the environment on the child and the child's individual response to it ... The teacher has to be prepared to follow up the personal interests of the children who ... follow divergent paths of discovery.' (Plowden Report, 1967, vol. i, p. 200)

But, as we have seen, it is not 'the direct impact' of the environment which initiates interest. Many of children's 'individual responses' to such 'impacts' are not 'interests' at all. Even if they were, however, it would be both foolish and wrong, and probably impossible anyway, to allow children to 'follow' them all. Reading the above passage one can visualize with great clarity groups of H.M.I.s following children up hill and down dale on 'divergent paths of discovery', through bush and through briar, careless of all merely prudent or moral considerations, let alone of educational ones. Alternatively one can imagine a complete paralysis of action when *all* the children attempt to start following *all* of their 'divergent paths' at once. Either way, it is inconceivable that such 'newer methods', described at least in theoretical terms of this kind, could be responsible in practice for guiding any 'particularly good work'.

'Good work' does no doubt exist, but this passage from Plowden is an example of the kind of theory which gets in its way, not of the kind which guides it. Before such a theory could be constructed, first a much clearer connection must be made between interests and values, and then between both of these and education. In the meantime it is plain that of the interests which children would *like* to follow, many are wildly imprudent, many trivial and many ill-chosen on moral grounds; and that in any case they cannot *all* be followed at once. Some selection, then, *must* be made. It is the problem of finding educationally good grounds for such selection with which I am concerned in each of the two parts of this final section of the present chapter.

(a) *Interests and values* In order to do more than scratch the surface of this topic, I must take up again the question of the relationship of 'needs', 'interests' and 'reasons for action' upon which I have already touched in section 2 of chapter 1 and also in section 2 of the present chapter.

Both 'needs' and 'interests' may furnish 'reasons for action', but, logically speaking, they function in language as 'reasons' of two entirely different sorts. For example, 'needing fish' is one sort of reason for going fishing; 'being interested in fishing' is a reason of a different category altogether. Either or both of these reasons may *explain* the actions in which I am engaged here and now, such as checking my lines, stocking up with bait, getting the boat out. But the existence of a reason for action, although always sufficient to furnish an *explanation* (or a partial explanation) of the action, is not always sufficient to *justify* it, even partially. 'Needing fish' could partly explain why I am going fishing, but if by going out and *buying* some fish I could give myself time to do any number of other things which are more urgently in need of doing, then going *fishing* for fish would not be justified at all; and we would say, then, that 'needing fish' was not a *good* reason (just now) for going fishing. By contrast, at *any* time at all, 'being interested in fishing' not only explains why I am going, but also functions as a justification (or a 'good' reason) for doing so. Here and now, of course, there may be *better* reasons for doing something else. If I have a heavy cold at the moment, for example, although 'being interested in fishing' would still be a sufficient justification (or 'a good reason') for going, it would probably be *better* not to. On the other hand, however, if I merely *need* some fish, and if I could meet this need just as well by telephoning the fishmonger, then 'needing fish', by contrast with 'being interested in fishing', would not in the circumstances be 'a good reason' for going fishing *at all*.

It will be true to say, then, that in the sense which I have described, a child's interest will always constitute 'a good reason' for engaging in the activities which he sees as relevant to it. It should be equally plain, however, that on *other* grounds, unconnected with that interest, there may be *better* reasons for his not engaging in such activities at all, or at least not doing so for the time being or in the present circumstances. Hence, to say that it is good for children to be able to 'follow their interests', is true if by this we mean that engaging in interesting activity is always something for which the presence of the interest constitutes 'a good reason'. But it is *not* true if by it is meant that the presence of interest is always the *best* reason for action (other things considered), or that the things which children are interested in are always the best possible things for them to do—and it is this interpretation of the connection of 'interests' with 'reasons for action' which is suggested, unfortunately, in the passage from Plowden quoted above.

Readers should explore for themselves something of the background of the topic of 'reasons for action' by consulting, for example, Taylor's *The Explanation of Behaviour* (1963), or chapter 6 of White's *The Philosophy of Mind* (1967) or the first two chapters of Peters' *The Concept of Motivation* (1960). In the meantime, let me try to put my point about 'interests' and 'reasons' in another, and possibly more familiar, way.

Whenever the word 'need' is used in referring to a reason for action, it is implied also that reasons can be given *for the need*. Not only does the 'need' point to a reason for the action; *beyond the action* there exist also reasons for the need. For example, if I say that I am reading a certain book because I 'need' to check my recollection of a particular point in its argument, it is implied (by my use of the word 'need') that reasons exist, in turn, for my need to check my recollection. Indeed, if you questioned me further, I might be able to give quite a number of such reasons. I might explain, for example, that I have a poor memory and therefore *always* 'need' to check back to the original source in order to be sure of a point. Or I might say something about why I 'needed' on the present occasion to refer to *this* particular point, or why I particularly 'needed' on this occasion to be *sure* of this point ... and so on. In this way, with you questioning and me answering, a dependent chain of 'needs' may be revealed, or in other words a chain of 'reasons for' my action in reading the book. *Beyond* my reason for reading the book, therefore, would lie a range of further reasons *extrinsic* to that activity. Beyond the activity of reading the book would be a logically interminable sequence of activities, the performance of each one a possible prerequisite to the performance of the next.

'Needs' are 'reasons for action', then, only *because* someone (and not necessarily the person 'in need') can point to extrinsic reasons *for the needs*. By contrast, although 'interests' are 'reasons for action' too, this is not *because* of any extrinsic reasons which there may happen to be *for those interests*. By pointing out extrinsic reasons for an interest (or 'the source of a proneness', in White's phrase), such as for example the circumstances in which it first arose, one would not be doing anything to justify its pursuit. To give *good* 'reasons for action' in pursuing it, the most that one could do would be to try to explain to the questioner the *intrinsic* reasons for its interest, or in other words to *teach* him exactly what it was which one was finding interesting *in* it.

For example, then, if you ask me on another occasion why I am reading a certain book, and if this time I give as my 'reason for action' that I find it extremely interesting, it would make no sense for me to try to explain this further by telling you what it was interesting *for*, or what is interesting *about* it. It might for instance have been written by a friend, but this would not be a good reason for *finding* it interesting, though it might of course explain why I first began reading it. The only good reason for *finding* it interesting *is* its interest—and this is a reason intrinsic to the activity of reading the book, not to the fact that it happened to have been written by a friend. Therefore, if you persist in wanting good reason for my action in reading the book, then I can do no more than try to teach you what *I* find interesting in it—the humour of one of its characters, for example, or the subtlety of its plot, or the surprise of its ending, and so on.

'Interest', then, by contrast with 'need', is always 'good reason' for action; and, if all that we are concerned with is the possible value or good *intrinsic* to an action, then the child should 'follow his interest' and we should help him. But if we are concerned also (as we almost always are) with values *extrinsic* to that action, then we must weigh up whether there are not also other and *better* reasons for putting a stop to it, at least for the time being. If the child's interest seems a comparatively trivial one (e.g. wiggling his ears), although its interest is sufficient both to explain and to justify his effort in trying to learn how to perform the appropriate action, there may be other things which he would be *better* occupied in doing. If his interest seems likely to prove extremely harmful to himself or others (e.g. dropping lighted matches into a tin of paraffin), then again, although his finding it interesting is 'good reason' for doing it, there are *better* reasons for his not. Finally, if his interest is morally obnoxious (e.g. tormenting an animal), then although the animal's unhappy antics are unfortunately 'good reason' for tormenting it, on moral grounds there are *better* reasons for saying that it ought to be stopped.

To sum up: 'needs' *presuppose* values; 'interests' do not. I 'need' to go fishing *if* I am to achieve a particular valued goal to which fishing is a means, and *if* (moreover) I could not achieve this goal as well or better in any other way (such as going to the fish shop). But there are no 'ifs' about 'being interested'. My interest in fishing is not conditional upon my valuing anything *other* than fishing. By saying that I find interest in fishing, I am saying that I find in it something of intrinsic value. There is always value, therefore, 'in' my interest, even though what I value may turn out to be utterly worthless in terms of anything *else* than its interest, and even though the pursuit of it may be positively detrimental to the achievement of *other* valued goals. In the second part of this section I shall argue that the educative task of teachers is to help children to understand more fully and to practise more effectively *some* of the things which they find interesting, and thus to get a measure of the value intrinsic to them. But to advocate learning, in this way, 'through interest' is not to give *carte blanche* to the assistance of *all* the multitudinous and often nefarious interests which any particular child has. In practice even the child himself has to choose which of his interests to follow at any particular time. *Helping* him to choose sensibly, in terms of the keenness and clarity of his interest, the availability of resources for the pursuit of it, and the compatibility of this pursuit with other equally interesting pursuits, is just as much a part of educative teaching as is the help which the teacher should give in the actual pursuit itself. Over and above such *educational* grounds for selection, however, teachers have a duty, too, to consider whether or not a particular interest is undesirable on *other* grounds, such as its being very probably dangerous, or being morally obnoxious.

(*b*) *Interests and education* What I am advocating here has often been called 'child-centred education', but a teacher who stands back and just *allows* children to pursue whatever interests come into their heads is practising, as I have argued elsewhere (Wilson, 1969), a travesty of 'child-centredness'. The feature of the concept of education which 'child-centred' educators were concerned to stress was its connection with the development of whatever is of intrinsic value, and thus, in the case of children just as much as in the case of adults, its connection with the notion of 'interest'. The point of calling education 'child-centred' lies in emphasizing that even when the person who is being educated is a child, and even, therefore, when his interests often seem 'childish' or silly or undesirable from the point of view of his adult teachers, nevertheless his *education* can only proceed through the pursuit of his interests, since it is these and only these which for him are of intrinsic value. However ridiculous a child's interests may seem, there is nothing else in terms of which he can become *more* 'educated'. He can be 'schooled' to adopt adult values, but only at the expense of leaving his own in their present childish and uneducated state.

A person's interests, dispositional and occurrent, represent his capacity (such as it is) to find intrinsic value in the circumstance of living, and his inclination to pursue or seek such value in terms of feeling and understanding and of activity which seems appropriate to its practical point. Such a person's 'education', I believe, whether in or out of 'school', consists in whatever helps him to develop this capacity for valuing and this inclination to pursue what is valued. Thus, whatever enables him to appreciate and understand his interest more fully, and to pursue it more actively and effectively, is 'educative'. But this does not mean that teachers, even when they are thinking about 'educating' children rather than just about 'schooling' them, should give assistance in the pursuit of anything and everything which catches the interest of a particular child. Still less does it mean that they should stand aside, or merely 'follow' the child down 'divergent paths'. There is a difference between helping a child to follow an interest *for* himself, and abandoning him to get on with it *by* himself. A merely tolerated child is apt to wonder in the end what his teacher is doing at school at all, if all that he ever hears from that teacher is 'Yes, Billy. On you get with it, then.' Ultimately Billy will be bound to start asking what *teacher* is 'getting on with'. Meanwhile, the interest which he had been casting around for ways of pursuing 'appropriately', founders for lack of help.

There is a constant risk involved in pursuing an interest, since no one can ever say in advance exactly how it is going to turn out. In it, one is not trying to approximate to a *norm* of action, or in other words to do what the majority of people might agree that one 'needs' to do. It is not a matter of trying to conform to *proven* or *consensual* standards or norms of value. It is more like trying to find out more about what it is which gives value *to* norms, or like *seeking* a measure of value against which to *evaluate* norms. In principle, this is a risky business. There might turn out to *be* precious little value in the direction in which we have taken it to lie. Or, in gaining what is of value in an interest, we might lose other values which previously we had achieved in other directions, or jeopardize the future achievement of further values in store. Just as each new understanding which we gain restructures our entire conceptual grasp of the world in which we live, so each new value which we find or seek, in pursuing an interest, brings about a shift —and sometimes a radical shift—in our entire current *scale* of values. Such changes, although pursued for their interest, are by no means always in *our* interest, let alone in the interest of anyone else. The inherent uncertainty of life's outcomes is what makes possible its interest. It also makes unavoidable its risk. Children, therefore, and perhaps especially children educationally speaking, need constantly the kind of confidence to proceed which comes from receiving effective help. This effective help is the educative function of teachers, and it *includes* the weighing of each risk against its possible gains.

By contrast, then, with the kind of manipulative changing of behaviour which I described in section 4 of chapter 1 and in section 3 of the present chapter, 'teaching' of an *educative* kind consists in helping children to structure their experience and activity in ways which enable them to see more of its intrinsic point and value. Once again I am making many assumptions here, both about 'values' and about 'teaching', which the reader would do well to explore more fully, for example by studying Taylor (1961) on 'values' and Bruner (1956; 1961; 1964; 1966a; 1966b) both on 'values' and on 'teaching'. What I am trying to suggest, however, is that children benefit 'educationally' by *learning* how to pursue their interests both more effectively and in an increasingly selective and discriminating way, and that 'educative teaching', therefore, is whatever intentionally serves to bring about this end. ' "Ought",,' as philosophers would say, 'implies "can"' (e.g. Henderson, 1966; 1969), but not everything which *can* be done *ought* to be done. It would be unintelligible to say that a person 'ought' to be interested in *anything,* unless from time to time he were inclined already to see intrinsic value in *something*. But this means only that a sense of the intrinsic value of *some* thing or things in life cannot be induced in people solely by manipulating the external conditions in which they live. It does *not* mean that anything and everything which a particular person values is *bound* to prove valuable or to be most worth pursuing here and now.

A child's interests are already selective. Through them he begins to discriminate intelligible and possibly valuable features of the world. Trying to pursue an interest means always, then, trying to see those features more and more clearly, and in doing so, *trying out* (as it were) their possible value. The child's *educational* need is to be sustained and helped through these trials, so that his interests neither become fixed in some stereotyped form through his inability to see how to develop them further, nor remain at the fleeting level which, by themselves, his own unaided efforts might achieve. But neither on educational nor on any other grounds does the child 'need' to pursue *all* his interests. Indeed, it is only on educational grounds that he 'needs' to pursue *any* of them. There is room, then, for other grounds such as prudence, practicality and morality to be considered, when the selection is being made as to which of his interests should be pursued in school.

If *only* these 'other grounds', however, are being considered both by children and by teachers, then school becomes a place where no education can possibly be going on at all. If one were *always* to be prudent, it would be unwise *ever* to pursue an interest for its own sake, because of the *unavoidable* risks involved. A school staffed by teachers who are never more than prudent becomes, therefore, a sort of value-dump of supposedly good things whose *intrinsic* value is the one feature of them which no one can ever afford to consider. The prudent children, meanwhile, become artists in strategies for *concealing* their interests from adults whom they know, from bitter experience, will merely make use of those interests for well-intentioned but unintelligible purposes of their own. The child's own culture or sense of values, such as it is, is the price which he is required to pay, in such schools, for the acquisition of adult norms. There is no other reason for his going to school, in that case, than that he must.

3
Discipline

1   *The morality of compulsion*

Thus far I have argued, all too sketchily, that it is the interest of school which forms the necessary, though not the sufficient, condition of there being 'good reason' for children to go there. Some apparently interesting pursuits are impractical, others imprudent, others immoral—and the occurrent interest of school, therefore, is not a *sufficient* condition for saying that children should go. It is, however, a necessary condition. If school were *never* interesting to children, then, however useful it might be as a prerequisite for the attainment of 'desirable' ends, in itself it could be of no intrinsic value. It could not be right, therefore, to say that there was 'good reason' for the children to go. One could say on other grounds, perhaps, that reasons existed because of which they *needed* to go, but this would not make it right to say that therefore they necessarily *should* go. 'Needs', as we have seen, ultimately presuppose the existence of intrinsic values. One could never show that an action was *right*, then, merely by pointing out things for which it was 'needed'. Only if there were something intrinsically valued *in* school, and only if we sent children there because of it, could it therefore be morally as well as educationally justifiable (or 'right') to say that they should go.

The first step, then, in trying to ensure that children go to school for good reason, is not, as has often been done, to dream up a list of morally desirable goals and then to search for methods of making schooling an efficient means to their attainment. The first step is not a moralistic one at all. It consists in trying to ensure that the life which it is intended that children should be able to live in school *is* actually a life which will be of occurrent interest to the particular children concerned. Only then could one be in a position to argue that there were *moral* grounds for saying that children should go to school.

I turn now to the second of the two questions which I raised in my Introduction (see pp. 2-4). Granted that logical conditions can be specified for the moral justifiability of saying that children *should* go to school, why, morally speaking again, should they *have* to?

Once again the issue, I must stress, is a logical, not an empirical one. Trying to resolve it is not a matter of looking about for some set of circumstantial *facts*, because of which one might argue that it would be right for the children to have to go to school. There exists no set of circumstances which makes the compulsion *right* (if it is right). Certainly facts exist because of which we can say truly that children *do* have to go—legal facts, economic facts, social facts and so on. But the existence of these facts is not something fixed and unalterable, like the 'fact' that 2 and 2 make 4 or the 'fact' that the sun rises in the east. The circumstances because of which in our society children *do* have to go to school, unlike the 'facts' of logic or of nature, to some extent at least are deliberately contrived and therefore avoidable. The children's 'having to go', then, cannot be *justified* by pointing out 'the facts'. On the contrary, in the last resort it is only if the children *should* have to go that the avoidable existence of such facts is itself morally tolerable. Just as, for example, a state of national emergency such as a war would *explain* (but not by itself *justify*) various compulsory constraints such as conscription and occupational redirection, so the existence of certain laws, certain vocational requirements and a certain social class structure in our society help to explain why children *do* have to go to school, but say nothing at all about why they *should* have to (if, indeed, they should). If it is true, then, not only that they should but also that they should *have* to go, then in both cases the use of the word 'should' must be a moral one.

My argument in this chapter and the next, then, will be that the morality of compelling children to go to school is something which (if it exists at all) derives logically from the morality of the practice of schooling itself. Only if in practice a school *is* a place to which we can rightly say (for the sort of 'good reasons' sketched above) that children should go, can we *also* rightly say that they may justifiably *have* to go. To put it another way: if *in practice* a school is of the sort to which children should go, then and only then can it be true also that they should have to go—not

because the law says so, or because it will keep them out of mischief or out of harm, or help them to get on in life or to adjust to
society, nor because it will (or may) lead to any other circumstantial
gain to themselves or to others, or even to some other morally
desirable end, but because it is part of the logic of the word 'should',
when used in a moral sense, that when we say that something
'should' be done we imply that it would be true to say that it is
right for us to *have* to do it. The compulsion to do something moral
is implicit in the *morality* of doing it. In the words of R. M. Hare:

> ... to say that moral judgments guide actions, and to say that
> they entail imperatives, comes to much the same thing. (1952,
> p. 172. See also 1963, ch. 5.)

In the case of schooling, then, the compulsion is no less moral,
and no *more* moral, than the schooling itself. Instead of saying that
children should go because they 'must' (in the sense of 'needing to'
on extrinsic grounds), I am saying in effect that *if* they should go,
then—morally speaking—they *must*.

Let me try to approach this controversial and difficult conclusion
from a slightly different angle. If school were a place where one did
not ever have to do one sort of thing rather than another, or where
in other words just anything (or nothing in particular) went on,
there would be no point in saying that anyone *should* go there. One
could do nothing in particular just as well somewhere else. Again,
if one were free to go or not to go to school merely if one felt like
it or as one pleased or on impulse, then there could hardly be any
point in saying that it was the sort of place to which one ever
should go. Similarly, there would be no intelligible point in saying
that teachers, rather than, say, child-minders or caretakers, *should*
be employed at school, if it were *only* a place where everyone
could do as they pleased or just play about all day. But if it is true,
on the other hand, that it is ever morally justifiable to say that
children should go to school, then it must follow that school, in
that case, *must* be a certain sort of place—a place in which both
children and teachers will 'have to' be doing certain sorts of things
rather than others, in order for there to be any *intelligible* point in
saying that they are doing what they 'should'. The presence of
'teachers' implies a curriculum for learning, and a curriculum implies some systematic limitation of both teachers' and pupils' activities in which some things 'have to' be done and others do not.
But the compulsion, where it is justifiable at all, is a *moral* com-

pulsion. It exists, when it does exist, only because it is logically entailed in the *moral* judgment that school is a place where pupils
and teachers 'should' go.

The question of the morality of compulsion lies at the heart of
the problem of discipline in schools. Centrally its difficulty stems
—as does much of the difficulty which besets educational theory—
from the fact that the problem itself is a particular formulation or
version of a much more general problem, central to moral philosophy. Trying to understand (as we are now) the morality *of* compulsion in the particular context of schooling is but one instance of
the difficulty of understanding the compulsion *in* morality in
general.

One could ask the same question about life in general, in other
words, as about schooling. Why (in any situation at all) should
one *have* to do what one should do? or, what *makes* a moral situation 'moral'? or, what *is* a 'moral' compulsion? This is the general
question which one faces at the *end* of moral argument as to what
one should do: granted that I should do X, in what sense do I 'have
to' do it? Thus, for example, Paul Taylor raises this question at the
end of Part I and again in the final chapter of his book on *Normative Discourse* (1961). Baier asks it at the very end of *The Moral
Point of View* (1958), as does Toulmin at the end of *The Place of
Reason in Ethics* (1950). In philosophical journals, of course, there
is a steady stream of discussions upon it (e.g. Ralls, 1966; 1969), and
not surprisingly, then, it is a question to which one is bound to
receive a perplexing answer.

Such discussions are not simply about why one *should* do what
one knows that one should. To ask this would only indicate one's
confusion about the meaning of the word 'should'. Rather, the
question is about the sense in which one *must* do what one knows
that one should. Specifically, is it a *moral* sense, or not? Personally,
I know of no system of moral philosophy in which an adequate
answer is explicitly given. As Beardsmore has put it recently:

> The majority of moral theories can be seen as attempts to find a
> middle term which will connect reasons and conclusions in a
> moral argument. (1969, p. 71)

What, then, is the *force* of a moral argument? Once we have
reached our conclusion (e.g. 'Children should go to school'), then
no doubt this conclusion is morally binding upon us. If we are to
be moral, then we will have to act in accordance with our con-

clusion. But were we *morally* bound to reach such a conclusion? If we were not—if our conclusions were for instance *psychologically* determined, or if they were deductively entailed by the existence of some set of unevaluated 'facts'—then how can we be sure that our conclusions were indeed 'moral' ones? To put the question in the terms made familiar by Hare (1952, chapter 4), how can we make principled 'decisions of principle'? Upon what *principle* can we decide to adopt one 'principle' rather than another?

In this book I am committed in the last resort to the sort of answer, as I see it, which Hare gives to the question. If I am to agree that I must do as I know that I should, this will not be merely because I happen to prefer to see things in this way, or because I have some sort of faith that in this way everything will be all 'right' in the end, or that my decision will tend towards the greatest 'happiness' or the general 'good' of all. My decision must rest ultimately on my preparedness in practice *to be bound* by that decision : to act on it, to suffer the consequences of it and, in short, to try to live by it. This is the discipline or 'sting' which, as Hare says, lies in the tail of any *moral* decision (1952, p. 69). Further than this also, however, it seems to me that to say that I am prepared to be bound morally by a decision to do X, and to say that I take X to be of intrinsic value or that I am prepared to attend to it for the sake of *its* interest (rather than my own or someone else's), are sayings of an equivalent kind. Of course, I would not agree that I was morally bound to pursue *all* that I find interesting, since one interest might for example conflict with another. But *unless* I saw something of intrinsic value in X, or could see something of *its* interest, I cannot imagine that I would be prepared to bind myself to a decision to treat it as something for the sake of which I should try to act in the way appropriate to *its* interest (rather than to mine or to someone else's).

My conclusion then is that the force of a moral decision must derive ultimately from the interest which one finds in trying to live according to it, rather than from anyone's pleasure, happiness or any other 'good' to which it may contingently prove conducive. In schools, then, the children's discipline must derive ultimately not from empirical considerations or calculations (by the children or anyone else) of ways in which to obtain or produce 'goods', but from the moral compulsion implicit in their own interest *in* the school activities themselves. The question of the compulsion of the children *arises*, therefore, when their interests are being lost sight of, either by the children alone, or by their teachers too. In the former case, the compulsion can be a matter of disciplining interest; in the latter case, where no effort is still being made to find out what the children's interests are, to educate them and to foster new ones, the compulsion can only be manipulative and psychological—a kind of motivational leverage brought to bear *upon* the child in order to control his behaviour in desirable ways of whose intrinsic value he has no inkling himself. However 'good' the ends for the sake of which the child is thus compelled to 'behave', he does not benefit *morally* from being made to pursue them. In the terms which I have been using throughout, he becomes better 'schooled', but not necessarily more 'educated'; and in the terms which I have introduced above and which I shall try to clarify in the remainder of this chapter, he becomes subject to 'control', but not thereby more 'disciplined'.

But, it may be asked, why do interested children ever *need* 'disciplining'? Surely, one might think, if they are interested in an activity, they will be eager to get on with it. Why should they ever have to be reminded or prompted or even deliberately 'ordered' to tackle it, for example, in a sensible rather than a silly way? Why *do* they ever 'lose sight of' their interest?

This question again illustrates the intimate connection which this whole topic has, as I said earlier, with the general problems of philosophy. In its general form it is one which has been written about under the title of 'backsliding', for example by Hare (1963, chapter 5; 1952, p. 143, p. 169, etc.). If there is something which one should do, and if one *knows* that one should do it, how does it ever happen that one becomes liable nevertheless to go off and do something else? Similarly, if there is something in which one is interested, and if one can *see* the interest of it, how does it ever happen that one fails nevertheless to sustain the effort necessary to pursuing that interest in the 'proper' or 'appropriate' way?

Of course, in the light of what Piaget has written about children's moral and other reasoning, it may be doubted whether they ever *do* 'know' what they should do or 'see' what is appropriate to the pursuit of their interests. Certainly, if (below a particular age, at least) they were incapable of *any* sort of moral or other reasoning, then, on my analysis, they would be ineducable and it would at least not be *wrong* to treat them like little machines, plants or animals. Similarly, if below a certain age they were incapable of seeing *anything* of the rational import of a situation, they would be incapable of pursuing an interest in a manner in any sense 'proper' or 'appropriate' to it, for they would be incapable of seeing what was 'appropriate' and what was not. But should we interpret Piaget's findings in a manner such as this? Isn't it precisely *because* children find it difficult (but not impossible) to grasp reasons, after a fashion, that there is some point in trying to help them to learn to do it better? Similarly, isn't it *because* they are liable at times to 'lose sight of' their interests and to pursue them foolishly or not at all, that the *education* of those interests can sometimes be a going concern? The special feature of 'interest', by contrast with other sorts of inclination such as 'likings' and 'impulses', *is* its cognitive character or, if you like, its 'teachability'. It is an inclination not just to have fun with the interesting object or impulsively 'do' things with it, but to pay attention to it, *looking for* appropriate forms of relationship with it. But, at whatever age a particular child may in fact be deemed capable of having such an inclination, no one (adult or child) ever *does* everything which he is inclined to do. An interested person is *inclined* to do what is appropriate to his interest—but he doesn't *always* do it. Similarly a moral person, or one who is *inclined* to do as he should, may sometimes fail to do so.

In order to 'pursue an interest', a child *must* (logically) be prepared to look for some kind of orderly limit within which, so far as he is capable of seeing, that interest may be appropriately pursued. Of course *his* idea of 'appropriateness' will not be shown in a form identical with that of an adult, but it will have to make *some* sort of sense consistent with (or at least not logically incompatible with) others' ideas of any interest which both they and he claim to share (see my discussion of 'appropriateness' earlier, in chapter 2, section 2a). He is not 'playing football' if he behaves in a way which makes it impossible for anyone else to play. He is not appropriately 'looking after a pet' if he swamps it in food one day and then starves it for a week. He is not 'reading a book' if he is just holding it up in front of his face while he chats to a friend. *If* he claims to be interested in 'playing football' or whatever it is, then he must be *prepared* to submit to the discipline of trying to understand what is appropriate to that interest, and what is 'appropriate' will be something in which others who share his interest will be as entitled (but not *more*) to have a say as he is himself. The understanding of this will not be an all-or-none affair which he will 'have' at one Piagetian stage and be totally incapable of at another. It will be gradually and effortfully *learned*, with much 'backsliding' along the way.

With recurrent puzzles such as these, then, in mind, I shall continue in what follows to try to contrast more clearly what seem to me the two distinct and different ways in which we try to *teach* children to do what they should. The distinction, I shall argue, lies between on the one hand behavioural control through fear of penalties and hope of gains, which merely 'schools' children to believe that what is most valuable is what most nearly approximates to norms settled almost entirely for them by others, and, on the other hand, the intrinsically rewarding and punishing (or 'disciplinary') process of trying to find ever more appropriate ways of viewing what they themselves find interesting and therefore take to be of value.

2   Discipline and control

Both discipline and control are forms of order, but the order in each case is of a logically different kind. In the former case, the order in a 'disciplined' activity is achieved by virtue of reasons implicit in, or for the sake of values intrinsic to, the activity itself. In the latter case, the order of a 'controlled' activity or sequence of events is achieved for reasons unconnected with, or for values extrinsic to, the activity. Thus, a 'control' is a way of ordering things which is considered necessary for getting something done. By contrast, a 'discipline' is the form of logical and evaluative order which must be learned if one is to understand what is involved *in doing* something. Both control and discipline involve compulsion, but in the former the compulsion is not in the first instance a logical or a moral one. It is not achieved through the force of a logical or of a moral imperative. The force is physical, as when we arrange for things to be physically manipulated in certain ways (the 'controls' of an aircraft), or psychological, as when we employ psychological sanctions to ensure that people or animals behave in certain ways (police 'control' of traffic, military 'control', the 'control' of the lion-tamer over his troop). In discipline on the other hand, the compulsion involved has nothing to do with the physical and psychological force which backs orders and instructions in the sense of commands. When instruction enters into the achievement of discipline, it is 'instruction' in the sense of teaching, not in the sense of giving orders. When we 'order' or 'instruct' someone *to do* something, as in giving commands, we are not *teaching* him what to do. We are just *telling* him.

When we exercise 'control' over people, therefore, we are not 'disciplining' them. The question 'Who is in command here?' or 'Who is in control here?' means 'Who is responsible for getting things done in this situation?' It does not mean 'Who is getting the people here into a disciplined frame of mind?' 'Control' over people is a way of deliberately *putting* them in an order designed or intended to accomplish some purpose to the achievement of which (*in* that order) they are merely a means. By contrast, when we 'order' dinner we do not think of ourselves as *controlling* the waiter, and we do not feel that we are being 'controlled' by the instructions (the informative directives) on a packet of cake-mix or in an AA route-guide. This form of order (in serving dinner, making a cake, getting to Brighton) is not achieved merely by submission or obedience to orders in the sense of commands, but by trying to see what the *point* of the orders is. It is a matter of discipline, or in other words of trying to learn what is involved *in doing* what is being ordered.

Similarly, when we talk of a teacher 'controlling' his class or of his class 'controlling' him, although a form of order is present in both cases, in neither case are we talking about 'discipline'. In so far as the relationship between teacher and class is simply one of means to ends, in which each tries merely to get the other *to do* something, then each purpose is accomplished at the moment when, willingly or unwillingly, the other *does* it. It is quite irrelevant whether or not the children (or the teacher) can see the intrinsic point of what they are being ordered to do, so long as they *do* it. When the teacher commands the class, for example, to sit down, stop talking, be quiet, pay attention, listen carefully and so on, there is no clue *in* his commands as to what the point of obeying them could conceivably be. If *all* that the teacher is trying to do (at the start of a lesson, for example) is to 'gain control', then he is almost bound to fail to bring the class to order. If he is to obtain more than momentary and unco-ordinated obedience, his children must be able to see something of the point *in* the order for which he is asking. As students find out to their cost when they are advised to get the class absolutely quiet *before* they start teaching, if one merely *orders* quiet, one may wait for ever. It is impossible to get thirty or forty children simultaneously quiet for more than a moment or so unless *they* can see some point or value in the constraint. 'Getting the class quiet' is a matter of discipline, not merely of 'gaining control'. It is not something to be done *before*, but rather is *part of*, 'starting to teach'.

It is a mistake, I think, to contrast discipline not with control, as I am trying to do, but with order (as in for example Harold Entwistle's *Child-centred Education* (1970, p. 67), since discipline is itself a form of order. Similarly, it merely confuses the issue, it seems to me, to speak of control metaphorically as 'external' discipline, since the whole point of the term 'discipline', as I am using it, is that the orderliness characteristic of it is 'internal' to the activity or relationship in question. A disciplined relationship between teacher and class is one in which *both* parties to the relationship (the teacher as well as the class) submit to the educative order of the task in hand. The 'discipline' is not something which one party to the relationship possesses *over* or manages to impose *upon* the other. Unless the person being disciplined, as well as the one doing the disciplining, can see at least something of the valuable point of the proposed order, then he will not submit to it for *its* sake (for its *intrinsic* value) but only, if at all, for the sake of values 'external' to it. In this case, to say that he is being 'externally' *disciplined* sounds to me like a contradiction in terms. It would be clearer to say that his behaviour was being *controlled* by considerations external to the logic of the task in hand. Thus, if a child tried to get his sums right *only* because he valued the gold star which his teacher would then give him, I would not call the relationship between teacher and child a 'disciplined' one. Instead I would say that the teacher was 'controlling' the child, and that the child was 'controlling' himself, through the desire for gold stars. By contrast if the child had understood something of what 'right' means, and had seen, therefore, that there is no point or value *in* (or intrinsic to) the activity of 'doing sums' *unless* one is trying to get them 'right', then I would call his effort to get his sums right a 'disciplined' one.

Discipline, then, is educative order. The word 'discipline' refers always to the kind of order involved in trying to reach appropriate standards or follow appropriate rules for engaging in a valued activity. The valued activity may be a very personal one; it might involve the learning, even, of an entire way of life (as in 'disciple-ship'). It may be a highly intellectual activity (as in the 'discipline' of different forms of thought such as history and mathematics), or a practical or an aesthetic or a moral one. The point in each case, however, is that *any* valued activity, so long as it is distinguishably

79

one activity and not another (and so long, therefore, as there are discoverable rules and standards proper to it), *must* be engaged in in a more or less disciplined way if it is to retain its interest. The sense of the word 'must' here is not the commanding or manipulatory sense which has its proper place within a system of control. It is the logical or moral sense which belongs in the setting of educative teaching and learning.

Unlike control (whether 'self-control' or 'external control'), discipline does not involve the setting up of some previously non-existent order, or the gaining of regulative powers over something previously regulated differently or not at all. It involves getting to understand *more* of the sort of order which is already more or less explicit in what one is trying to do. One does not 'set up' the disciplines involved in something like mathematics, as one 'sets up' a system of control. The features of mathematics in virtue of which we call it a 'disciplined' study are already, as it were, 'there'. They are not 'there' or in existence in the sense, however, in which the hider in a game of hide-and-seek is 'there'—'ready' to be 'discovered'. They are 'there' more in the sense in which America was 'there' for Columbus—little more than a direction in which to travel, towards a form or shape of things only partly understood. If one is interested in the study of mathematics, having some inkling of what it is about, one is then concerned to become further instructed in it and hence to discover more of those special features in virtue of which it is the sort of study which it is. Receiving such 'instruction' does not consist in obeying commands which contain no clue as to the point of the order being asked for. It consists in trying to understand the *informative* directives with which the teacher helps his pupils to see more explicitly the 'form' or order of the mathematical task or situation which they find interesting.

Similarly, one does not set out to 'get' discipline *over* other people or *over* oneself, though one may try to gain control in this way. A disciplined social group does not behave in a disciplined way *because* someone in particular is in control over it or has responsibility for it, but because its members are themselves concerned to discover increasingly the features in virtue of which it *is* the particular and distinctive group in which its members are interested. If they share no interest, they cannot become a more disciplined group. Their 'discipline' is the educative order in virtue of which there continues to be some distinctive and intelligible point in their existence *as* a group.

3   Discipline and prudence

Now, as I tried to explain in the previous chapter (see pp. 49-53),
neither we nor the child can ever be *certain* whether his interest
may not be largely spurious—a protective mask or disguise for
something else—or whether it is genuine but still relatively
ignorant, having *something* distinctive and orderly about it, even
though this is still only very partially understood. As I indicated
in my examples on p. 76, one criterion of the child's interestedness
in something will indeed *be* his willingness to seek various forms
of order in its pursuit, by trying to engage in it in a disciplined
way rather than just by doing things impulsively, or for fun, or
only so long as he likes them. In the same way, perhaps his willingness when challenged to try to explain (or show) what he is doing
and to give (or show) reasons, as he sees them, for doing it in that
particular way, may be a further criterion of the genuineness of his
interest.

In the last resort, however, what makes the reasons for his
activity intelligible *is* his interest. Unless we are at least *trying* to
share his interest, we will be incapable of understanding his
reasons. If we press his reasons far enough, ultimately all that he
will be able to say (or that his behaviour will show) is that *this*
is what he finds interesting. It would be a mistake, therefore, to say
that if there seems to be no *further* reason for his acting in that
way than his apparent interest in doing so, then it cannot be worth
his doing. It is precisely at this point, indeed, that his educational
need is greatest for some instructive help *in* doing it. Yet it is at
this point, too, that we are most likely to abandon our effort to
share and help him in his interest, about which we know so little,
and to prefer schooling him in our own (about which, by comparison, we probably know so much). In other words, it is when
we, too, seem to be missing the point of his interest that the
educative order of the situation is liable to break down and we are
apt, therefore, to substitute some form of control. 'Leave that,' we
say; 'it's not getting you anywhere. Come and do *this*.'

Of course, if we are *sure* either that there is *harm* in what he is
doing or that absolutely no progress is possible in it in the present
circumstances, then plainly we are right to put a stop to it, at least
for the time being. But on what grounds should we be sure? If our
only reason for calling it 'harmful' is that it seems imprudent by
current *general* norms of health and harm, rather than by our

particular judgment as to its possible health or harm *in this instance*, and if our only reason for seeing no 'future' in it is that it does not happen to belong to what is currently on the list of things *generally* considered worthwhile for children to do in school, then, in either of these cases, it is certainly not necessarily our duty to stop the activity, neither, as educators, would we be right to do so.

I remember occasions on playground duty, for example, when boys used to ask permission to go along the top of a twenty-foot wall, down a sloping roof and into a courtyard, to collect footballs which sometimes got kicked over there. General standards of health and harm are quite inadequate in such a situation, so long as one is thinking in terms of what children find interesting, as well as of what is 'normally' in their interest. In practice, of course, I looked round for a boy whom I *judged* could cope. But if I had *only* been prudent, I doubt if I could have allowed anyone ever to go at all.

The situation is no different in principle from that in which one has to *judge* whether a child should take one course of study rather than another. To continue with the one in which he is most interested may often be altogether imprudent, in terms, for example, of his future examination performance. Yet to go on with the subject which may be *vocationally* more rewarding may, just as often, put an end to his *education*, at least so long as he remains at school.

It would be a mistake, I am suggesting, to confuse those occasions on which children *have* to be controlled, with those in which both they and we are learning to think about something in a more disciplined way. The control of children could never, so far as I can see, be something which helps to *initiate* them into thinking in a disciplined way. What interests children is not something which we can control 'externally' (or which they can control 'internally'). On the contrary, it is *because* they find some things interesting that we *can* control them at all (by controlling the conditions under which we permit them to pursue those interests). To the extent that they are already interested in something, they are already thinking about it in a more or less disciplined way. Our educative task, then, as distinct from but not necessarily opposed to our prudential task in controlling and schooling them, is to help them to elaborate and differentiate the disciplined character of the thinking which they are *already* engaged in, in the pursuit of what they find interesting.

On this view, whether the actual activities in which pupils are engaged are cookery, gardening, mathematics, cricket, hopscotch, wall-climbing, history or anything else, is of no particular *educational* significance, any more than it was *educationally* significant that it was America, not some other place, which Columbus happened to discover. One might be concerned about pupils' activities on *other* grounds, such as whether they were dangerous, for example, or involved harm to others—and on these grounds one would *have* to exercise some control over the activities and the pupils. It would be absurd, for example, to let a child dash across a busy street in front of traffic merely on the *educational* ground that he was extremely interested in something happening on the other side of the road. Nevertheless, in advance of knowing which activities were interesting to pupils, one could never rule out any activity at all on the grounds that it was inherently *uneducative*, nor could one have any *educational* ground for declaring that there are some things rather than others which all pupils, regardless of their interests, *must* study.

4 Worthwhile activities

It is at this point, perhaps, that there is some conflict between the view of education which I am describing and that of R. S. Peters, although just how fundamental this conflict may be I am still not altogether sure. (The matter is discussed in Wilson, 1967; Peters, 1967b.)

It is, he says, because some activities rather than others best exemplify or most explicitly embody disciplined, rational inquiry, that we should place these activities compulsorily at the centre of the school curriculum for all. The very fact that we are concerned to give good reasons for a curriculum is itself the best possible reason for getting pupils going on those theoretical pursuits such as science and history in which the different forms of disciplined thought can be seen (by us, at least) in their most highly developed state.

Whenever a teacher or a pupil starts to think seriously about what he is doing (as he *must* start to think, if he is going to engage in it in a disciplined, educationally worthwhile way), then, argues Peters, he is bound to find himself involved in the sorts of intellectual pursuit of which ultimately (as we, at least, can see) the curriculum of a university is largely constructed. Thus, he says:

> It would be irrational for a person who seriously asks himself the question 'Why do this rather than that?' to close his mind arbitrarily to any form of inquiry which might throw light on the question which he is asking. (1966, pp. 162-3)

Therefore, he argues, if the curriculum of any child's schooling is to be *educationally* justifiable, it must include those intellectual pursuits which *we* can see as best exemplifying the giving of good reasons for *anything*, even if at first the children themselves, understandably, cannot see them in this way.

If the kind of compulsion which is being envisaged here is logical, or in other words if all that is being said is that *any* serious thought is *logically* bound to take more or less orderly and intelligible forms, then I am not sure that the conflict between what is being said and the principle of 'learning through interest' is a fundamental one. Unfortunately, however, the argument can also be interpreted (White, 1969) as meaning that all pupils must compulsorily be *made* to undertake studies such as science and history seriously—and the compulsion intended here is psychological and perhaps, if necessary, physical. This compulsion, it is argued, has a prudential function, as a prerequisite for the pupils' eventual attainment of a worthwhile way of life. In no other way, the argument runs, could we be sure that *all* pupils would have the opportunity to develop the capacity (eventually) for making rational choices about what they should do when (eventually) the compulsion is lifted. Not before this point (i.e. eventually) would it be rational to free them from external compulsion.

But obviously one aspect of the problem here is to find a *rational* way of deciding what is meant by 'eventually', or in other words of deciding *when* it would be rational for the external compulsion to be withdrawn. Plato, for example, seemed to think that it could not be before the age of about fifty or so that people (and then only a very few people) would be able to make rational choices and, therefore, would be fit to graduate from the ranks of the compelled to join the ranks of the compellers. This, of course, was just Plato's opinion. There is no rational way of *knowing* whether or not a person has become capable of rational choice. One could never be sure on *rational* grounds alone that one's criteria for judging rationality were themselves rational and were being rationally employed.

Further than this, however, from what I have already written it should be plain that there is something very odd about the whole idea of proposing to use physical and psychological sanctions to 'make' pupils undertake certain studies seriously, just as there would be about trying to 'make' them interested in something by such methods. One can compel someone's obedience to a system of social control, but no one can be *psychologically* or *physically* 'made' to submit to the *logical* and *moral* imperatives of disciplined thinking. It would be like standing over someone with a stick or a threat of imprisonment and saying 'Will you or will you not admit that 2 and 2 make 4!' or 'Will you or will you not admit that one should pursue truth!', and continuing in this way until (eventually) he was 'forced' to admit it. It may be an empirical question whether or not, and in what precise circumstances, anyone subjected to such treatment ever *does* subsequently become interested in or start to think seriously about the matters which he has first been, as it were, force-fed. But at least it should be clear that the force-feeding, in itself, does nothing to help the pupils even to *start* to understand or see the intrinsic point of the subject-matter. I cannot see anything *rational* about my trying to force someone to study seriously the things which *I* take seriously and see as best exemplifying rationality but which *he* as yet does not. On the face of it, indeed, I would think that such treatment would be at least as likely to close his mind to those things as to open it. To offer him some extrinsic reward for studying or to threaten him with a penalty for not studying might, indeed, be the very thing most likely to convince him that there was no *intrinsically* good reason for such studies, and that the real reason for undertaking them must therefore lie in their contingent utility for getting pleasures and avoiding pains.

Moreover, it is in any case one of the main theses for which I have been arguing that there is no *educational* need to treat pupils in this way, however necessary it may seem at times on grounds of prudence. And, on balance, I think that this argument, rather than such arguments for the compulsory curriculum as those of J. P. White to which I have referred, is supported by the main part of what R. S. Peters has written on the subject. (For a fuller critical assessment of White's viewpoint, see Thompson (1970), together with the subsequent correspondence in *New Society* between Thompson and White.) What has been shown, I believe, by Peters is that a more or less disciplined understanding of *whatever* a pupil is engaged in is an essential part of what we mean by the educativeness of a situation. His argument, as I see it, is not that children need to be forced to 'study science', for example, because then they will *get to think* rationally. Rather, it seems to me, he is saying that 'studying science' is one of the things which we *mean by* 'thinking rationally'. It would follow, then, that to the extent that a child was engaged in *any* activity in a way which involved trying to think about it rationally, he would thereby *unavoidably* be engaged in thinking about it 'scientifically'. If this were so, then the issue turns on how narrowly or widely one limits or defines the activities which one is prepared to count as being bona fide examples of 'thinking scientifically', 'historically', 'mathematically', 'aesthetically', 'morally', and so on. Differences of definition in this case, however, would be stipulative, not a matter of differences of fundamental principle. An infant school and a university teacher might have differences, for example, about what they were prepared to call 'art'. Both, however, could still agree as to the seriousness, and therefore the more or less disciplined, rational and educative character, of their pupils' thinking.

To me it would seem then that what has been established is that a child does not have to be made to wait until he has studied certain school subjects as defined, say, by university teachers, before he can be adjudged to be (more or less) rational. If he is seriously studying the doing of *anything*, then he is engaged already in trying to be more rational about *it*. If his teacher, in separating out the logically distinct forms of thought which the child is actually developing in this way, finds it helpful to use, or to avoid, labels such as 'science', 'history' and so on, this does not affect the basic issue of principle which is involved, nor should it be allowed in any *further* way to put limits on what the child *must* do if he is to succeed in his activity. If a child is interested to find out more about how his family, for example, or his neighbourhood or school or anything else, got to be the way it is, whether or not one calls this 'studying history' is not the vital issue; and to try to compel him to undertake such inquiries because one considers it vital for him to 'do history', would be a pointless undertaking. What is of fundamental importance educationally is whether or not his inquiries (whatever they are) are being engaged in for their intrinsic interest. What makes his curriculum educationally worthwhile is not the presence on it of any particular school subject, but the presence *in* it of serious thought about *whatever* he is doing.

'Serious thought' means thought for which one is prepared to give one's reasons, up to the point at which there are no more reasons which one can give. At this point one can and should be willing to be instructed, but, educationally speaking, no one can or should try to psychologically or physically *make* one receive that instruction. To see the point of an instruction one has to be trying to do so. One cannot be 'made' to see its point by being instructed *to do so*. The only way in which one could interpret such *un-illuminating* instruction ('Do it *or else!*') would be as a series of commands to be obeyed.

5 'Disciplines' and 'subjects'

In the present chapter I have tried to explain my view that whereas 'instructing' in the sense of commanding or 'giving orders' which are backed by psychological and physical sanctions has no place at all in educative teaching, instructing in the sense of 'informing' is an integral part of such teaching. It seems to me misguided, then, to try to restrict instruction, as many teachers do, to certain 'compulsory' subjects or to the so-called 'basic skills', while *depriving* children of educative instruction in other areas. Usually this deprivation is called 'leaving children free to discover', and, apart from 'discovery learning' in mathematics and science, the areas in which children are commonly left to flounder about by themselves in this way are those of the so-called 'practical' and 'creative' activities or 'topics'. Where instruction is unilluminating, naturally enough it must seem to the child to be no more than a stream of arbitrary constraints. On the other hand, when children *do* find instruction informative, their being given it does not somehow make them less 'free' or in some sense imply that they have been prevented from 'discovering' its significance *for* (as opposed to by) themselves. Logically speaking, one could never 'discover' something which was *totally* 'unstructured', inchoate, formless—for in a formless experiential flux there would be nothing 'there', so to speak, to 'discover'. Aside from that, however, when pupils *do* grasp the illuminating point of instruction it makes perfectly good sense to say that *they* have thereby been helped to 'discover' or 'find' its relevance or connection with whatever it is which they are trying to do. One of the main values in having a good teacher, I would have thought, is from the child's point of view that with his instructive help interesting activities and experiences do not remain in a *relatively* formless, incoherent, 'unstructured' state.

I am not concerned, therefore, with the relative merits of 'instruction' and 'discovery learning' as *alternative* methods of teaching (Dearden, 1967), since I do not see them *as* alternatives. What seems to me of main importance, rather, is the dependence of *both* of them, if they are to be educative or in other words to help children to make any progress in the pursuit of their interests, on the selection of appropriate subject-matter for study in school. If the teacher is preoccupied, above all else, with getting the children to study certain 'subjects' whether they find them interesting or not, then, where there *is* no interest there will *be* no 'illuminating point' in his instructions, since there will be nothing in the pupils' experience for those instructions to connect with. Similarly, if he abandons explicit instructions in favour of 'discovery materials' intended to get the children going on those subjects by themselves, the children in this case will still not have the faintest idea what it is that they are supposed to be 'discovering'. In neither case can the situation become an educational one. The children's 'practical activities' remain on the undeveloped level of more or less fleeting and pointless amusements or diversions. Little serious thought goes into them, because no effective help is being given about *how* to think about them in a more disciplined and effective way. Where there is *no* intrinsic connection between the teacher's preoccupations and the children's interests, probably the most that the latter will 'discover' is that school is a place where it pays you to *look* as though you're seriously busy, regardless of whether you yourself can see the point of what you're doing or not. Meanwhile the teacher expends *his* effort in securing obedience to his instructions, or attention to his 'discovery materials', generating theoretical pursuits whose practical point may be clear enough to *him*, but could never be clear to the children except in some more or less remote and eventual future.

The content of the particular 'fields of knowledge' (e.g. Hirst, 1967; 1969) as one actually finds it in 'school subjects', is arrived at chiefly, I would think, on the *practical* grounds of its interest to the people engaged in teaching it. What concerns me is that these practical grounds are seldom the pupils' ones. More often they relate, for example, to particular academic traditions and to the examination requirements by means of which teachers test knowledge of those traditions. What I am suggesting is that in many cases the teacher's overprotective attitude towards or preoccupation with his own 'discipline' and his concern with getting pupils to pursue it in the way, eventually, in which he would like (or would have liked) to pursue it himself, is educationally speaking misplaced. To the extent that a child is 'thinking seriously' at all, rather than acting merely on impulse or from liking or for immediate gratification or to please or placate (or annoy) his teacher, then it seems to me that it is *logically* unavoidable that his thinking will come increasingly to take conceptually distinct 'forms'. But these categorial or conceptually distinct 'forms', increasingly explicit in disciplined ways of thinking or 'forms of thought', are not somehow paradigmatically embodied in 'school subjects' or in 'fields of knowledge' as these are found in school curricula. What particular children will think seriously *about* is something which we cannot forecast or preselect with any reliability until we ourselves are taking an interest in and 'thinking seriously' about the practical pursuits of those children. This is something which we scarcely ever do, since the main part of our effort goes into devising 'methods' and 'materials' for getting the children, theoretically at least, to engage in *our* favoured pursuits.

It does not seem to me, then, that we have good grounds for saying that there are *some* activities ('doing' history, science, research, and so on) about which one can 'think seriously' and other activities (e.g. keeping pets, playing hopscotch, cooking, telephoning a friend) about which one cannot really 'think' in an educationally worthwhile way at all. Whether (for economic or other reasons) we call it 'work' or 'play' (Dearden, 1967; Manser, 1967), the 'seriousness' of any activity is shown by one's willingness to try to give reasons for the way in which one is engaging in it, or in other words by the extent to which one can show that one is thinking about it in a more or less disciplined way. For example, the *moral* seriousness of a game (*any* game), as something to be played 'properly' rather than just 'played about' (or fooled around) *with*, seems to me a far better guarantee that children will be likely to exert themselves in 'serious' thought about it (Wilson, 1968), than that provided by the vocational or economic or other 'good' reasons with which we so often try to persuade children to 'work'.

Practical considerations can be placed first, then, in planning school curricula, without this endangering in any way the disciplined character of pupils' thinking. But the chief practical consideration for the teacher, in my view, should not be his respect for his *own* characteristic style of thinking (nor that of the academic tradition in which he sees *himself* as working), but for the pupil's. The pupil's thinking, too, has a tradition, and, unless the teacher begins his instructive communication with the pupil in a language and in relation to experiences and activities which *already* the pupil understands something of the point of, then no conceptual development and no development of interest will result directly from the encounter. To quote Bernstein again:

> If the culture of the teacher is to become part of the consciousness of the child, then the culture of the child must first be in the consciousness of the teacher. This may mean that the teacher must be able to understand the child's dialect, rather than deliberately attempting to change it. (1970, p. 120)

'*May* mean' is the understatement of the year: this is what it *must* mean. Moreover it must mean that the culture of the teacher, too, must change, at least until it reaches a state in which he is prepared to admit that the child *has* a 'culture', or in other words is something more than a mere barbarian at culture's gates.

To 'think seriously' is to ask oneself and others just *what* it is which one is trying to do and *whether*, therefore, it is being done appropriately or properly. One's capacity for 'thinking seriously', in this sense, depends not on any purportedly 'serious' quality peculiar to some activities and pursuits rather than to others, but on the quality of one's involvement in *any* activity or pursuit, or in other words one's interest in it for its own sake. Different people can be involved in entirely different ways in what is seemingly the same pursuit (e.g. 'studying' history). Whether pupils are thinking seriously about what they are doing will depend far less upon its theoretical or intellectual character, than on whether or not they are finding any point in thinking seriously *about anything at all*. If their occurrent interests are never 'seriously' considered by adults, if all questions of value except trivial ones are settled for them by others, and if they are never encouraged and helped to think things out for themselves as though *their teachers*' as well as their own values were sometimes at stake, then being prompted or stimulated to engage in theoretical or 'thoughtful' pursuits will not in any sense be equivalent to engaging in 'serious thought'.

'External' compulsion in schooling is needed to the same extent that children *do* need controlling and looking after, or *do* need adjusting (for their own sake as well as ours) to the most inflexible aspects of our social and physical world. Where such adjustment and control cannot be clearly shown to be necessary on grounds of prudence in an individual case, *there* is room for someone to help children to learn to do things in an increasingly flexible and thoughtful way. The only kind of compulsion appropriate to education, then, as opposed to schooling, is not that of control and command but that of discipline and instruction. Separating thought from activity—doing up 'thoughtfulness' in separate parcels of 'theoretical activity' labelled 'science', 'history', 'mathematics' and the rest—does not help children to be more thoughtful; and it more or less dooms the material in the *other* parcels (labelled 'practical activity', 'creative expression' and so on) to being engaged in in a thoroughly thoughtless way. Peters' arguments in the last two sections of chapter 5 of *Ethics and Education* (1966) do not seem to me to entail, on educational grounds alone, that we should rule some activities out of the curriculum and rule others in. Ordering someone to study something seriously does not help him to answer the question 'What should I do?' It merely settles it for him, making it at the same time increasingly pointless for him to think about *any* activities seriously at all. The thinking has been done by the teacher. All that is left for the pupil is to obey (or disobey).

Apart from the writers whom I have mentioned thus far, it seems to me that much else of what has been written about discipline in schools (e.g. Stenhouse, 1967) is not really about 'discipline' at all, but about 'control'. The values of school activities are seen almost entirely in terms of values lying beyond and outside the school. In school, therefore, since there is little or no intrinsic point in what they are expected to do and thus little discipline *in* the tasks themselves, pupils stand increasingly in need of external pressures and controls. Set to study 'the tropical grasslands' or 'life in Tudor England' or 'tessellations' for no discoverable reason except that that is what is declared to be essential for 'doing' geography, history or mathematics, which in turn is declared to be essential for the living of some allegedly desirable form of life in the 'eventual' future, children are left to find what stray bits of fun they can while they compulsorily 'cover the ground'.

This 'fun', derived maybe from any immediately pleasurable or curious features of the syllabus, the teacher, or anything else which happens to be around, is entirely irrelevant to 'covering the ground', except as a welcome distraction. Teachers skilful at control use 'fun' to brighten the drudgery of their and their pupils' tasks. Teaching becomes a matter of pupil management. Discipline becomes 'internalized' control. Education becomes schooling. In spite of the hopeful signs which writers such as Bernstein have seen in some schools (1967), fundamentally the picture has not changed, I believe, from the one which Waller described nearly forty years ago:

> The real influence of the school rests upon the fact that it confronts the child with social situations of a certain sort and compels adaptation to them. (1932, p. 448)

'It is an accepted principle,' says Bernstein (1970b, p. 347), 'that we should work with what the child can offer; why don't we practise it?' We don't practise it, unfortunately, because we still don't accept it. The child is the barbarian at the gates. He must go to school to get what's good for him on our terms. If he does not see the point of this yet, then he'll just have to work at it. In the meantime he has nothing to *offer* us. How *could* he have? He is not yet 'educated'.

4
Punishment

1 Punishments as 'reinforcement'

I have tried to explain how in my view it could never be morally justifiable to say that children *should* have to go to school, if all that we mean by this is that children stand in some sort of personal or social need of submitting to the control of adults. Only, I think, to the extent that school is educative, or in other words to the extent that it helps children to engage in intrinsically valued pursuits, can we reasonably say that it is right that they should have to go there.

Next, having argued that discipline is therefore a kind of compulsion to which it is *right* that one should have to submit, I must make out a parallel case for saying that punishment is the infliction of a kind of pain which it is *right* that one should have to suffer, not for breaking the rules of a particular system of control, but for moral wrongdoing or in other words for faults of discipline. Of course, in the dictatorial administrative climate of many schools, where headteachers control staff without giving them any genuine share in the process of decision-making, and where teachers control children in the same way, 'punishment' (and 'reward') is usually identified *with* the apparatus of control. Unfortunately, too, in most theoretical discourse as well as in practice, the matter of punishment and reward, like that of discipline, has commonly been treated as though it were part and parcel of the business of control. This is true not only in philosophical writings, in which (as I shall explain in section 3 below) punishment has usually been viewed as an adjunct of *legal* control, but also in psychology, in which it has often been treated as part of the mechanism of conditioning and related kinds of *psychological* control. However, in schools and other institutions in which by contrast there is some mutual agreement on the intrinsic value of attempting to live and work together in an orderly way, the form of order therein envisaged is a moral, not merely a social, one. Accordingly its development is a matter of discipline, rather than of control, and it will be my argument in this chapter, therefore, that in such situations punishment and reward are educative, rather than mere inducements to toe the line.

Almost any current text in educational psychology will illustrate to the reader the conflation of discipline with control, and the complementary treatment of punishment and reward as though they were agencies of psychological manipulation rather than features logically implicit in the notion of 'discipline' itself. Thus Ausubel, for example, writes:

> By discipline is meant the imposition of *external* standards and controls on individual conduct ... When external controls are internalized we can speak of self-discipline; it is clear, nonetheless, that the original source of the controls, as well as much of their later reinforcement, are extrinsic to the individual. (1968, p. 459)

'Punishment', correspondingly, is just the pain or 'aversive motivation' which helps the individual to realize what these external controls are and which thereafter induces him to 'internalize' them, or in other words which teaches him to control himself rather than to go on suffering others to do this for him. (See op. cit., pp. 379-84.) Why the 'internalization' of external *controls* should be called 'self-*discipline*' (rather than self-control), and why discipline in the first place should be located in sources lying *exclusively* outside the individual, are matters which are never explained. The morally distinctive feature of discipline (namely, that it is a form of order which is sought for its *intrinsic* point) and of punishment and reward (namely, that they are the pains and pleasures which one *deserves*, rather than which it is merely expedient for one to avoid or to seek) play no part in the account.

Similarly Sears and Hilgard in the essay to which I have already referred (p. 54), describe reward and punishment as 'techniques of control' (p. 192). The employment of these techniques, they claim, is part of 'the teacher's responsibility for maintaining discipline in the classroom'. Pleasure and pain 'reinforce' learned behaviour, and reward and punishment are simply the deliberately administered positive or negative 'reinforcements' with which the teacher secures whatever kinds of behaviour he thinks desirable in the classroom. But in this account, too, once again no *reason* is given for equating discipline with control, or rewards and punishments with 'reinforcement'.

Just as 'learning through interest' rather than through extrinsic controls has so often (and so disastrously) been misinterpreted as meaning that such learning needs no discipline, so punishments and rewards have often been eschewed by well-intentioned teachers, as though they were matters which *had* to be construed as extrinsic 'reinforcements' and which therefore could *never* be intrinsic to the task of learning. At other times, on the grounds I suppose that it is somehow less indefensible to manipulate people in ways which they find pleasant than in ways which cause them pain, teachers have been prepared to 'reward' children, though not to 'punish' them. Thus many teachers have felt guilty about punishing their children for wrongdoing, and even at times about rewarding them for doing right, because they have been led to believe that such treatment is merely a kind of external manipulation or control which 'in theory' should not be necessary when children are 'learning through interest' or in other words are 'intrinsically motivated'. But all learning takes place in a social context. The pleasure of successful learning is as much social as intellectual in origin, as is the pain of failure. When children are 'learning through interest', then, as much as at any other time, it is absurd to try to keep them in some sort of social vacuum empty of both punishment and reward, or to place them in the kind of socially sterilizing situation in which, while behaviour which deserves to succeed is applauded, whatever is deserving of failure is merely ignored.

More recently, some psychologists have been coming round to the opinion that it may actually make some children *happier* to get 'punished' now and again, since maybe this satisfies their 'basic need' for security. Thus, says Ausubel for example:

> Without the guidance provided by unambiguous external controls they tend to feel bewildered and apprehensive. Too great a burden is placed on their own limited capacity for self-control. (op. cit., p. 459)

It is the helpful function of 'punishment', then, Ausubel claims, to make the external controls 'unambiguous' to the child, to help

> structure a problem meaningfully, furnishing direction to activity—and information about progress toward goal—in terms of what is to be avoided ... (ibid., p. 380)

But this account misses the whole point of the difference between a manipulative situation and an educative one. Both situations are to some degree orderly and rule-governed, and in both situations, naturally enough, individuals become 'bewildered and apprehensive' if the rules remain ambiguous and vague. But in the former situation the *only* guidance about the rules derives from the pains and pleasures arbitrarily associated with their infringement or non-infringement. In the latter situation, by contrast, both the pains and the pleasures stem in part *from* seeing the point or rightness *of the rules*. In a manipulative situation, in other words, the rules are only 'right' in the sense that you get hurt if you break them. In an educative situation, however, it is *because* the rules are right that it hurts to break them. The former situation, again, is 'manipulative' in the sense that there is nothing worth learning *in* it except that you will get hurt if you break its rules. What Ausubel calls 'direction to activity' stems entirely from considerations *extrinsic* to the situation itself. In the 'educative' situation, however, there exists the possibility of learning something of the *intrinsic* point or rightness of the rules which thus far appear to define it. Manipulative rules *have* no intrinsic point in the situation which they govern. This is why it is correct to call them 'external' controls. The 'internalization' of these controls, so that the individual now begins to manipulate or control himself without needing too often the *active* intervention of others, makes no difference to the logical status of the manipulative rules. If they had no intrinsic point at the time when they were being imposed on the individual by others, they cannot somehow *acquire* intrinsic point merely because the individual has now been induced to impose them on himself. They are the same rules. They have no more intrinsic point than they had before.

My argument in this section has been that educational psychologists in the main have misinterpreted the logical status of 'reward and punishment', and that this misinterpretation is linked with their tendency to see learning in terms of conditioning, discipline in terms of control, and education in terms of schooling. In a parallel way, then, they see reward and punishment in terms of 'reinforcement'. The newer trend in psychology, according to which negative reinforcements or 'punishments' are now seen to be as important to the child as positive reinforcements or 'rewards', although no doubt it will prove a great relief to teachers who need not any longer accuse themselves of professional failure if they find themselves needing to have recourse to 'punishment', makes no difference to the matter of principle which is involved. Whether one only 'rewards' children, or whether one 'punishes' them too, in either case one's action is manipulative and its pain or pleasure to the child is a 'reinforcement', rather than a moral desert, if the rules in question define behaviour which has no intrinsic point. Versions (other than Ausubel's) of the allegedly wholesome effects of negative reinforcement may be found for example in the articles by Bronfrenbrenner, and by Sears, Maccoby and Levin, in Maccoby, Newcomb and Hartley (1959). For an account, however, of the inadequacy of reinforcement theories in general as explanations of how individuals learn in the sense of *understanding*, rather than merely in the sense of having the patterns of their behaviour changed, readers should consult for example the first part of Chomsky's 'Review of Skinner's *Verbal Behaviour*', which is reprinted in DeCecco (1967).

2 Punishments and penalties

Both discipline and control, I have suggested, are forms of order, the difference between them lying in the kinds of value inherent in the structuring of situations which they seem to make possible. Educative order or discipline is seen as being of intrinsic value by those engaged together on any task in which they share an interest. Manipulative order or control, on the other hand, is not seen as being of any value in itself, but just as a more or less efficient means to a goal valued by the controller alone. A controlled situation, therefore, is regulated by concern for values *other* than those implicit in the situation itself. To say, then, that social control is the first step, as it were, towards discipline seems to me as misguided as to say that extrinsic motivation is the first step towards intrinsic motivation or that schooling is the first step towards education. In each case two *logically* different kinds of commitment are involved. One of them cannot somehow 'turn into' or be 'a necessary first step' towards the other. This is a logical, not an empirical, point— a matter of interpretation, not merely of 'fact'. Educational situations (on *this* interpretation of 'education') are *themselves* orderly situations. 'The first step' in one's education, having seen value to lie in a certain direction, is to try to take that direction *because of* its value, not because of some *additional* penalty or advantage which one wishes to avoid or to gain thereby.

It is a mistake, then, to think of punishment in terms of a *penalty* which one has to pay for trying to get a personal advantage over others by stepping outside the limits of social control. Just as a footballer is penalized for dangerous kicking or for trying to gain an advantage by breaking for example the offside rule, so punishment has often been seen as a way of compensating society for some against-the-rules advantage sought or achieved in the great social 'game' of life. You break the rules, so you pay the penalty (fine, etc.); this is your 'punishment'. But this sort of 'punishing' (or penalizing), although appropriate to social control, is not part of becoming more *disciplined* and should not, indeed, be interpreted as 'punishment' at all. When we read of a footballer, who has *already* been penalized by the referee in a match, *afterwards* being 'disciplined' by being called before the coach or manager of his club, *this* is where we feel that his 'punishment', properly speaking, will take place. Even if that punishment is marked publicly by the imposition of some *further* penalty, such as demotion to the reserve team, still, 'paying the penalty' and 'being punished' are two entirely different things. The first is a matter of suffering a compensating disadvantage for breaking the rules. The second is a matter of learning that breaking rules which one values *oneself* is not just something for which, if caught, one must pay, but something which, whether one is caught at it or not, is 'wrong' and therefore, morally speaking, *deserves* to fail.

Punishing and penalizing, then, should never be confused with each other. Their logical characteristics are quite different. For example, provided that a person is willing and able to pay the penalty, there is no reason for saying that he *should* not repeat an offence, if all that is going to happen to him is that he will be *penalized* again. A motorist, for instance, may calculate that the gain of parking on yellow lines outweighs in his case the disadvantage of paying the fine when he is caught. It may thus be perfectly reasonable for him to continue to commit the offence, so long as he is not caught too often. Moreover, if challenged, he will say that there is no reason why he *should* not repeat the offence, so long as he is perfectly willing and able to pay up when caught. He is not being 'punished', therefore, by having to pay the penalty, nor is making him pay the penalty a way of 'disciplining' him. Penalization is a mode not of discipline but of social control. The size of the penalty, calculated against the size of the gain, controls the number of times that this particular motorist will commit the offence. By contrast, if the motorist begins to feel that parking on yellow lines (or if the footballer begins to feel that deliberately tripping or injuring an opponent) is not just something which may be advantageous to him in terms of gains over penalties, but is also something which may be 'right' or 'wrong' in *moral* terms, then, even if the penalty which he has to pay is to him a trifling one, requiring him to pay it will be a disciplinary act which he will interpret as a punishment.

It is not the *pain* of punishment which makes it 'punishment', any more than it is the pleasure of a reward which is *sufficient* to make it a 'reward'. When we inflict pain on someone in a way which he regards as unjust or undeserved, he will see this not as 'punishment' but as spite, retaliation or revenge. But even when he sees the pain as a just one, unless it is given for something which he regards as *wrong* (rather than just illegal or against the authorized rules) he will construe it as a penalty, not a punishment. Similarly, to give pleasure to someone, if he had no notion that he deserved such a thing, will seem to him like flattery, currying favour or offering a bribe, not like a 'reward'. But again, even when he feels that there is an acceptable reason for the pleasure in terms of custom or precedent (as on his birthday, for example), he will construe it not as a 'reward' but as a gift. Only when deliberate pleasure-giving is for *moral* desert, is it properly speaking a 'reward'. Other sorts of deliberate pleasure-giving come under categories such as 'gift' or 'prize', or on occasion 'bribe' or 'inducement', and so on.

In the same way, although to 'reward' someone gives pleasure both to him and to you, there is no question of there being an *advantage* in it for either of you. Similarly, to 'punish' someone is painful both for him and for you, but not in terms of some *advantage* which either of you have thereby lost. On the other hand, to 'award' either a penalty *or* a goal *is* to give something of disadvantage or advantage to the players in the game; and any pleasure or pain which the players feel because of it, derives *from* the advantage or gain which has thus been given or taken away. Reward and punishment, however, unlike gains and penalties, are given and received only when people feel to some extent concerned *morally* in their own case. Just as discipline involves a willingness and concern to correct one's mistakes and seek the truth *for one-self*, so punishment involves *one's own* willingness and concern to see faults and suffer their correction. There are always three parties to a penalty, one of whom (namely the judge or referee) must not be in a position to gain or lose thereby. But in a punishing (or rewarding) situation there are only two parties to the relationship involved. *Neither* stands to gain or lose extrinsic advantage thereby, and *both* must take part in the moral judgment which occurs therein.

3   The legal view of punishment

Readers may find some philosophical discussion of this crucial distinction between punishments and penalties in for example Feinberg (1965), Manser (1962) and, rather less usefully, in Locke (1963). The philosophical literature on punishment, however, is enormous. Not an issue of a learned journal goes by without additions to the already great spread of words upon topics such as blame, remorse, forgiveness, atonement, guilt, expiation, mercy, retribution, deterrence, reform, treatment, reparation and the many other notions relating to the general theme (see for example the selective bibliography at the end of Acton's collection of readings (1969)).

Apart from its sheer bulk, though, the most striking feature of the literature is that almost all of it is concerned with punishment in a *legal* setting. H. L. A. Hart, for example, explicitly lists among the five elements in terms of which he defines 'the standard or central case of punishment', that:

> (ii) It must be for an offence against legal rules ... (v) It must be imposed and administered by an authority constituted by a legal system against which the offence is committed (Hart, 1968, pp. 4-5)

and he continues:

> In calling this the standard or central case of punishment I shall relegate to the position of sub-standard or secondary cases the following among many other possibilities:
>   (a) Punishments for breaches of legal rules imposed or administered otherwise than by officials (decentralized sanctions).
>   (b) Punishments for breaches of non-legal rules or orders (punishments in a family or school). (ibid.)

But how can we hope to understand the place of punishment in education if in the very definition of it the educational case is regarded as sub-standard? Even in the few papers in which punishment *is* considered in other contexts than the legal one (e.g. Mc-Closkey, 1962; McPherson, 1967), the distinctive meaning of punishment in family and school situations is seldom pressed very far.

It has been taken furthest, perhaps, by McPherson:

We do talk of parents punishing their children, and we do talk of self-punishment. To say or imply at the outset that these uses are at best secondary or sub-standard is, even when a disclaimer is made, to depreciate any contribution that they may be able to make to the clarification of the concept of punishment. (loc. cit., p. 23)

As he points out later:

Punishment can turn up in any human relationship. Lovers punish each other, parents punish their children; the State punishes criminals. (ibid., p. 26)

It is exactly in the last of these examples, or in other words in the State's treatment of criminals, that 'punishment' comes closest, I think, to being nothing but an adjunct of social control, in the sense of being little more than the imposition of a set of graduated *penalties* for breaking rules devised not for persons in particular but for people in general (or 'in the general interest').

Trying to explain the meaning of 'punishment' by looking at it as exemplified in a court of law and its associated *penal* institutions, is like trying to paint a picture of something which one has seen only through the wrong end of a telescope: the vital details are blurred or missing altogether. All those features of punishment which are clearest and which count for most in a personal relationship are at their most obscure and their least valued in law, for the law is designed for 'the general public', not for particular persons. It could not be 'law', if it had any particular person in mind. But the consequence of this is that all the things which are of most importance in personal relationships, and hence in punishment and reward, are exactly the things which can least be taken into account in law. Thus, for example, fairness is obscure in law: through the wrong end of a telescope what some see as 'considering extenuating circumstances', others see as 'letting the blighter off' or 'going soft'. Forgiveness is obscure: the guilty must pay their penalty, regardless of whether or not being found guilty has been suffering enough. Remorse is obscure: the offender is free when he has paid his penalty, regardless of whether or not he is yet conscious of having done wrong ... and so on.

No doubt courts are no longer the entirely barbarous places which they used to be, any more than schools are. But just as schools, rather than, say, families and friendships, are not the best places to look for paradigm examples of education, so courts of law are not the best places to look for the clearest instances of what is meant by 'punishment'. In many schools one may see little more, even today, than the unique being brought into conformity with the norm. Similarly in the processes of law, and in the legalized 'punitive' practices of teachers, often little more is discernible than an elaborate set of devices for protecting that norm. Small wonder, then, that both in schools and in courts there are movements afoot to 'abolish' punishment and to substitute psychological and sociological therapy and treatment.

What seems to me amiss, however, is not the social practice of punishment, but the almost universal view that the legal case is the best example of it. The crucial (and murky) distinction between 'civil' and 'criminal' law, for example, depends heavily on this view. Thus, to take an easily accessible account of the distinction, in Geldart's *Elements of English Law* (1911) occurs the following passage:

> The difference between civil law ... and criminal law turns on the difference between two different objects which the law seeks to pursue—redress or punishment. The object of civil law is the redress of wrongs by compelling compensation or restitution: the wrongdoer is not punished, he only suffers so much harm as is necessary to make good the wrong he has done. The person who has suffered gets a definite benefit from the law, or at least he avoids a loss. On the other hand, in the case of crimes, the main object of the law is to punish the wrongdoer; to give him and others a strong inducement not to commit the same or similar crimes, to reform him if possible, and perhaps to satisfy the public sense that wrongdoing ought to meet with retribution. But this punishment is not directly or mainly beneficial to the person injured ... (pp. 154-5, 1966 edition)

From this it may seem at first as though the distinction is much the same as the one which I have been trying to draw between 'penalizing' and 'punishing'. For 'civil' wrongdoing, it appears, the law merely penalizes people; for 'criminal' wrongdoing it punishes them. But the whole point of the distinction which I had in mind is that one is 'penalized', not for wrongdoing necessarily, but for advantages gained through breaking authorized rules. Not all rule-breaking is wrongdoing. Only when the rules are *moral* ones does the breaking of them constitute doing *wrong*, and the distinction between a moral and a non-moral rule is not something which can be decided by any process of *law*. To put it another way, it is not a *legal* question whether an action in fact constitutes 'punishment' or 'redress'. What decides the matter is the *moral* judgment of the persons concerned.

What I am saying, then, is that very often, although 'the law' may claim to be punishing a person, what happens is that he is merely penalized for breaking a rule which he personally does not regard as a moral rule at all, or for the breaking of which he does not personally see himself as being morally responsible. In such cases, the penalty which he is made to pay *may* act as 'a strong inducement' not to break that rule again, or in other words as a sort of 'negative reinforcement', but, even if it happens to have this effect, this does not alter its logical status from that of a penalty to that of a punishment. Again, taking Geldart's second criterion, in a sense the penalizing of the rulebreaker *may* 'reform' him, if it happens in fact to 'induce' him to behave differently in future, but, even so, no 'reform' in the sense of a revision of his *moral* standards has thereby necessarily taken place. The individual may merely revise his *behaviour*, so as to avoid being seen to break that rule in future. Finally, if the third object of 'criminal' as opposed to 'civil' legal action is 'perhaps to satisfy the public sense that wrongdoing ought to meet with retribution', as Geldart rather uncertainly says, then civil redress, which according to Geldart is undertaken because a *wrong* has been committed, should be no less 'punitive' than criminal punishment. To say, as Geldart goes on to say (p. 155), that civil 'wrongdoing' involves 'merely an injury to an individual', whereas criminal 'wrongdoing' is 'a matter of public concern', is very odd indeed. In a moral community, injuries to individuals *are* 'matters of public concern'. It would be a very strange 'retributive sense' which was aroused by 'wrongdoing' in one case but not in the other.

For reasons such as these, then, it seems to me misguided to look at the processes of the law for the paradigm cases of punishment, because the law makes no *logical* distinction between penalizing and punishing—and merely *legal* distinctions are quite inadequate. Civil law, according at least to exponents such as Geldart, is not even *concerned* with punishment, but only with the restitution of social order or in other words with the maintenance of the status quo through social control. Criminal law, on the other hand, although it is *said* to be concerned with 'punishment', turns out instead to be concerned merely with the control of a special class of social rulebreaking—and a very ill-defined one at that—namely, the one which is 'a matter of public concern'. The law, therefore, in both cases seems fundamentally an agency for the preservation of a particular social order. Punishment, by contrast, is primarily a *moral* matter. Thus, to talk for example of 'abolishing punishment' in courts of law would mean proposing to abandon any attempt to treat the courts as agencies of moral education and to concentrate there, instead, upon the psychological and sociological control of social rulebreakers through the provision of therapy, treatment and welfare (see, for example, Wootton, 1959). But 'punishment', in that case, would still continue to exist, both outside *and* inside the law courts, to the extent that people in *any* situation continued to show a moral concern for each others' actions. Punishment is not something which can be 'abolished', any more than it can be created, *by law*.

Nevertheless, as I said at the beginning of this section, most of the philosophical literature on punishment continues to treat it in a legal setting. Controversy centres chiefly, therefore, on the question of which of the three criteria enumerated for example by Geldart (deterrence, reform, and retribution) is of most importance. Readers may gain an idea of the chief protagonists' arguments by referring to Acton's volume, already cited. In my view, however, by far the most coherent and systematic account of punishment in the legal setting is Hart's. In many respects it is similar to the less complete discussions by Quinton and by Flew which are available in Acton (op. cit.) and by Benn and Peters (1959, chapter 8; Peters, 1966, chapter 10). In what follows, however, I shall for brevity refer to it as 'the Hart account'.

4 Retribution, deterrence and reform

The crux of the Hart account is that there are really *three* accounts (not just one) which should be given of punishment. These should specify (1) what it is, (2) what it is for, and (3) who should get it, how, and how much; and these three separate descriptions would thus refer, respectively, to the meaning (1), the justification (2), and the distribution (3) of punishment.

One could give similarly itemized accounts (in theory, anyway) of *any* social practice—schooling, for example. What is it? What is it for? Who should get it, and how, and how much? The first two questions are theoretical, the third practical. What is characteristic of the Hart account of the social practice of punishment, however, is that each item is treated as being entirely separate from the other. Thus the different traditional 'theories of punishment' *all* contribute to the different sorts of answer which, according to Hart, are needed for the three separate questions. Retributive and utilitarian theories answer, respectively, the theoretical questions (1) and (2); and both retributive *and* utilitarian theories answer separate aspects of *each* of the three parts of the practical question (3). What do these terms 'retributive' and 'utilitarian' mean here?

In the first place, the popular notion of what is meant by 'retribution' confuses it with revenge and spite, or perhaps, more literally, with retaliation—'an eye for an eye and a tooth for a tooth'. But retribution, unlike retaliation, spite and revenge, contains centrally the idea of giving back not just what one would *like to* but what one *should* give back, in response to someone's action. Retribution is the *just desert* of action. There is nothing necessarily *just* about taking 'an eye for an eye'. Some people for example might *have* only one 'eye'. But in any case, if someone hurts or injures you, although you might *want* to get literally even with him, to respond in a retributive rather than merely a retaliatory spirit you would have to be guided entirely by the rights and wrongs of the situation as determined by rules and standards *independent* of your own personal impulses and preferences. If someone hits you and you hit back, this is retaliation—'an eye for an eye'. But if someone does right and is rewarded, or wrong and is punished, this, by contrast, is probably what he justly deserves. The retributive view of punishment, then, according to Hart, is the only one which reveals what punishment *is* (and thus provides an answer to question (1) above). If you personally don't approve of the idea of acting in a retributive spirit—if, continuing to confuse retribution with crude revenge, spite or literal retaliation, you still think that there is something barbarous or inhuman about it—then either you must abandon (or try to 'abolish') the practice of punishment altogether, or you must be prepared to live with a perpetually guilty conscience, since, each time that you punish someone, it will seem to you that you are doing something barbarous and inhuman and therefore wrong.

Punishment *is* retribution for an offence. This, then, according to Hart, settles question (1). Questions about what it is *for* (2), however, are quite separate from questions about what it *is*. By contrast with its meaning (1), its purpose (2) is to prevent and deter offenders and potential offenders from committing (or committing further) offences, and even, hopefully, to reform offenders so that they no longer even *want* to commit further offences. Punishment does not *mean* deterrence or prevention or reform, as is popularly supposed. Whereas it is not possible (logically) to punish someone without thereby performing a retributive act, it *is* (empirically) possible to inflict punishment upon someone without thereby preventing or deterring people from further offences and even without reforming the offender in any way. In practice some people *do* go on repeating offences for which they have been punished. Perhaps this means that they have not been punished enough, or perhaps it means that they have been punished too much or in somehow the wrong sort of way, but, nevertheless, they *have* been punished, according to Hart, and therefore deterrence, prevention and reform are not what we *mean* by saying that they have been 'punished', or in other words they are not what punishment *is*. Instead, they provide the reason or justification for engaging in it, in terms of social control. There are of course many *other* kinds of social control which would or which might deter or prevent people from committing offences— shooting them, for example, or bribing them, or depriving them of something which they need. But punishment, although it, too, is a method of social control, is one which differs from other methods, according to Hart, by being retributive or in other words by trying to ensure that offenders are controlled by the imposition of *fair* penalties. Similarly there are many *other* kinds of social control which aim not just at deterrence and prevention but at reform— 'houses of correction', for example, or psycho-surgical and psycho-physical treatment, or social care and welfare which aim to eliminate some of the *need* to commit certain offences such as stealing. Again, however, although punishment according to Hart does indeed aim at controlling people by reforming them, it differs from other 'reformatory' methods, once more, by being retributive or in other words by treating people as being to some extent still responsible for their actions.

So far, then, we have a *theory* of punishment; that is, we have some answers of an entirely general kind to questions about (1) the meaning and (2) the purpose of punishment. These answers, however, being entirely general, provide only *general* guidance in deciding in practice what one should actually do in particular cases, and, indeed, in deciding in practice what *is* a 'case' for punishment (as opposed to a 'case' for one of the other forms of treatment). In practice, then, we must reformulate our questions and our answers to try to fit them to particular cases; and it is at this point (i.e. in practice) that difficulties for the Hart account most obviously begin to arise. In practice we must somehow *combine* prevention, deterrence and reform on the one hand, with retribution on the other, into a synthetic *judgment* as to what to do, and such judgments are bound to be problematic. For example, if in practice it were *only* a question of deterring and preventing people from offences, then perhaps we should 'punish' not only the offender but also, say, his family and friends, since probably this would add greatly to the deterrent effect of the 'punishment'. And second, we might find that we needed on occasion not only to 'punish' the guilty but also the innocent, since this would perhaps deter the innocent but tempted. And, third, very probably we should not bother about whether or not our 'punishments' were unfairly severe, so long as they effectively put a stop to repetitions of the offences.

In each of these examples, plainly, the deterrent and preventive *purpose* of the 'punishments' has unbalanced the retributive *judgment* as to what should fairly be done. On the Hart account, however, instead of being interpreted as showing the inadequacy of the theory as a guide to sound practice, our unbalanced practical judgments are taken to show merely how far short of the ideal our practice usually falls. Meanwhile, then, however idealistic our theory, in practice our actions remain continually at fault. To take just the three examples enumerated above, first, by confining offenders in penal institutions, whatever we say about this in theory, *in practice* we often 'punish' not only them but also their family and friends. Second, by taking reprisals against a whole class of children when we cannot locate the actual perpetrator of an offence, and by instituting punitive methods of control over a whole class or school whom we suspect of temptations to commit offences, *in practice* we 'punish' the innocent. Third, by making a penalty stiff enough in theory to deter anyone, *in practice* we are bound to make it unfairly severe for *someone*. In each of these cases in practice, then, we make nonsense of the *theory* of the retributive significance of the 'punishment' as being something which is morally deserved.

Moreover, because of the unfairness of our practice in instances such as these, unintendedly we often alienate from commitment to our norms the very persons whom (in theory) we are trying to reform towards greater conformity with those norms. It is not even certain, in other words, that our penal system succeeds in practice in its *primary* purposes of deterrence, prevention and reform, except of course to the extent that by being actually put away from society further crimes against society at large are for the time being made more difficult to bring off. Even this inefficiency of 'punishment' for its main theoretical purposes, however, is not accepted in the Hart account as being an argument against the *account*, but only against the *practice*. For this reason it further arms those who argue that it would be better therefore, ideally, to abolish 'punishment' altogether and to substitute other forms of treatment and welfare (see e.g. Samek, 1966).

These problems of distribution, which amount to problems of reconciling the utilitarian and the retributive features of punishment, illustrate the difficulties which we run into in practice when we try to use the Hart theory for guidance. The theory then proliferates into reformulations which aim to deal with each exception as it arises, or in other words it tries to lay down practical guidelines for making our 'punishments' simultaneously more efficient *and* more deserved. Thus, as practical maxims to guide the distribution of 'punishment' in particular cases, we should hold that it is best to try to be as *lenient* and to 'punish' as *infrequently* as possible, and indeed only as a last resort, since in this way we will cut to a minimum the risk of doing someone an injustice. This is only negative guidance, however, comparable as a piece of commonsense to advising someone to eat as little and as rarely as possible since there is always the chance of his food's being poisoned. When we *do* have to 'resort' to 'punishment', then we should punish in such a way, and with such severity, as will not *so* alienate the offender that our subsequent attempts to reform him will be frustrated by his resentment. For example we should give him a short, sharp shock whose sting will quickly fade. The surprise of it must be sufficient to catch his attention or 'stimulate his interest' in our subsequent reforming effort, but the hurt of it must be weak enough to encourage him to believe that we do 'really' have his interests at heart. Of course, if the penalty fails to hurt him *at all*, then it will fail in its deterrent purpose and cease to have any point. On the other hand, it would neither be fair nor would it prosper our reforms if the offender were to get the feeling that what we are 'really' after, in the last resort, is just to *make* him toe our line, by sheer weight of psychological or physical pressure.

Therefore, to continue with our proliferation of practical maxims, we must make the penalty 'fit the crime', not in the crude retaliatory sense of an eye for an eye, a murder for a murder, a rape for a rape, but in some *subtler* retaliatory (and, ideally, retributive) spirit which unfortunately is difficult to explain clearly but which has something to do with matching the 'seriousness' of the penalty with the 'seriousness' of the offence. For example, if someone takes our property, then we should take a *due* or equally 'serious' amount of his, on a carefully calculated scale of fines, or we should take away from him not literally his *property* but the 'due' amount of the *means* to property (such as his livelihood, his social good name, and his freedom of action). Similarly we must make the penalty 'fit' the *criminal*, as well as the crime. For example if he *has* no property, and if he has already *lost* his livelihood and whatever social credibility he might once have had, then it would be impracticable to impose a fine. Probably the only penalty he can still pay is to lose his freedom of action. However, if he still *has* property and can therefore be fined, the 'due' amount of the fine will vary, to some extent, in proportion to the amount of property which he has. In this way the fine will 'fit' the criminal. Again, if he has some sort of reasonable *excuse* for what he did, then, regardless of how much property he has, he will not *need* such a large penalty to deter him from similar acts in future, since he appears already to be to some extent motivated towards avoiding such acts. For example, if he exceeds a speed-limit while taking an injured child to hospital, then he should be let off with a caution or perhaps even exonerated entirely, depending on the 'seriousness' of the child's injury and the 'seriousness' of the hazard to others occasioned by the car's excessive speed. On the other hand if his reasons for the offence, although understandable, are entirely selfish, then he will need a 'serious' penalty to motivate him into avoidance of such actions in future. If he has *no* reasons, then of course he is a 'case' for some other form of treatment than the one which, in theory at least, is retributive.

These are the sorts of consideration to which in practice the theory gives rise and under the weight of which, in my view, before long it breaks down. Punishment, on the Hart account, is the 'fitting' penalty which those who are right (or have the right) *in law* are thereby legally entitled to exact from those who have done 'wrong' as defined *by law* (compare Hart, 1968, pp. 4-5; Peters, 1966, p. 268). If the law itself is sometimes wrong, then this is regrettable, and in due course better laws must be devised, but in the meantime we should not let occasional injustices cast doubts on the morality of the practice as a whole. Similarly, if pains and penalties are occasionally undeserved or not *exactly* 'fitting', and if unfortunately the innocent are sometimes 'punished', then this is not unexpected, and of course we must continue to work at making the system fairer without impairing its efficiency. But, in the meantime, we are doing the best we can. On balance, we cannot be blamed for trying.

Punishment, therefore, is at best an unpleasant nuisance (on the Hart theory), but it is not, as Bentham called it, a mischief, since its *purpose* is not mischievous but on the contrary is to motivate people into doing what is theoretically in the interests of us all. Its *intentions*, in other words, are good, and, even though the road to hell is in parts paved with them, it would be unfair to call good intentions 'mischievous'. Pain (to put the point another way) is evil, and therefore, as Bentham argued, the deliberate infliction of pain (as in punishment) is evil. Nevertheless, in punishing, we are *justified* in acting evilly, since we do so not out of a 'mischievous' intention but only for the sake of preventing the even greater evil of failing to enforce the law which in theory, if not always in practice, is in all our interests. To the extent that people remain 'evil', in the sense of being unwilling to obey the rules unless they get hurt when they break them, it is still necessary to employ that form of treatment or social control, namely 'punishment', which will 'teach' them to toe the line. *Other* forms of treatment, involving some surgical, chemical or electrical transformation of the individual, or some automatically regulated manipulation of the conditions in which he lives, should only be used when the rule-breaking person plainly cannot be expected to have behaved differently, or in other words when (through stupidity, mental illness, or severe social disadvantage) he is not in a position to learn from his mistakes.

5 The morality of punishment

In the Hart account, 'punishment' is a form of social control which, unlike other regulators, leaves the individual with a reasonable chance to control himself, by penalizing him when he does not. In the school situation, similarly, when 'punishment' is interpreted in this legalistic way, the child is not required to learn anything *from* his 'punishment', but only *because* of it. Its point derives solely from its social purpose, which is to induce the child to change his behaviour. When that has been accomplished the 'punishment' has served its purpose, whether it was deserved or not. Beyond that, although in theory it is always supposed to be fair, in practice it has no point. The child may therefore think and feel what he likes about it, so long as because of it he learns to make his behaviour conform to the external or behavioural order of school society.

By reading the Hart account for himself, the reader must judge the extent to which I have been fair or unfair to it in the above description. As an account of the institution and practice of social penalizing (or 'punishment' in the legal sense) it is unrivalled in its scope, completeness and detail. Yet, chiefly through consideration of the sorts of moral impasse to which I believe that it gives rise in practice, it seems to me that in its basic assumptions it does violence both to what punishment *is* and what it is *for*. In practice, in other words, I find that I am simply not prepared to believe that *all* punishment in school is no more than, as Peters puts it, '... at best a necessary nuisance' (1966, p. 279). On those occasions when it is not just an imposition of a penalty and when its purpose is not just deterrence, it seems to me that it is more than merely part of an unpleasant duty to make children suffer so that those who are not too silly or too disturbed will have the sense, out of self-interest, to control their own behaviour in future in more socially acceptable ways. I would agree with Peters (loc. cit.) that deterrents are necessary for order in school (as in society in general) and that having to impose them is a nuisance, when what one wants to do is to get on with the business of teaching. I would agree, too, that the imposition of deterrent penalties is not in *itself* of any educational value, but I would *not* agree that this sort of imposition is 'at best' what we mean by 'punishment'. Punishment, to me, is something educative. In it is revealed an entirely different dimension of value (namely, the moral dimension) from that which is bounded merely by fear of loss and hope of gain. It is not something which, like a necessary nuisance, we would avoid if we could. *If* we are to be moral—and there is no reason, other than a moral reason, why we *should*—then we must be capable of giving and of receiving both punishment and reward. Without these, a whole range of human experience, implied in terms such as 'forgiveness', 'remorse' and 'retribution', would remain meaningless or unintelligible.

For reasons such as these, then, I feel that I must part company with the Hart account. Philosophers, of course, have made numerous far more detailed and specific criticisms of various features of it, but these would deserve a separate book to themselves. Here, I can do no more than give the very briefest of examples and, in so doing, try to indicate something more of my own point of view. Predictably, perhaps, some of the principal criticisms have come from retributivists, such as Mundle, Mabbott, Armstrong (all reprinted in Acton, op. cit) and Ewing (1963), and, certainly, it is because it seems to fail to do justice to the retributive or 'morally fitting' character of punishment that I believe that the account is basically flawed. Yet retributivists themselves, notoriously, from Hegel and Bradley onwards, have failed to give adequate accounts of this elusive feature of 'moral fittingness' which is central to their theory. Indeed, they have sometimes seemed to be describing 'retribution' in terms which make it sound like a sort of moral medicine, which one must dutifully 'swallow', in order to get back into a healthy moral frame of mind. In this case though, as Mundle for example argues, retributive punishment is reduced once more to the status of an unpleasant social utility which one would avoid if one could. In other words it loses its distinctively *retributive* character as a morally intelligible response to wrongdoing and becomes merely a more or less efficient device for regulating conduct. But punishment is not something which for example one uses for 'generating remorse' as one retributivist has put it (Maclagan, 1939). 'Remorse' is not a *product* of punishment merely (see Thalberg, 1963). It is far more like a feeling that one has done something which deserves *to be* punished.

But this criticism still leaves the vital feature of 'deserving to be punished', or of punishment as something which is 'morally fitting', unexplained. And in general, unfortunately, it seems to me that 'retributivist' accounts of retribution are no more successful than that of the Hart account itself.

A second line of criticism, equally predictably, has come from utilitarians, such as Samek (whom I referred to above, on p. 108) and Thompson (1966). Here the argument has been that the Hart account, far from having failed to emphasize sufficiently the retributive character of punishment, has been wrong to give any emphasis or even credence to it at all. Sometimes, in the writings of critics such as these, it seems that Hart is being advised to forget about trying to make punishments *fair* and to concentrate instead on the real job of deterrence and reform—and certainly it is because of the conflict in practice between efficiency and fairness that, as I tried to point out in the previous section, the Hart account runs into difficulties. Extreme versions of this view, such as that of Smart (1961), even argue that on occasion an unjust punishment could conceivably have *more* of a deterrent effect (and would therefore, though unjust, be more justified) than a just one (see criticisms of this view by e.g. McCloskey, 1962). At other times, however, it seems that these critics are saying that we should stop trying to *punish* offenders at all, if by 'punishment' we mean some sort of retributive action. Thus, says Samek:

> What we need is a positive and comprehensive plan that will enable us to dry up the sources of criminality. Instead of punishing and making examples of offenders we could then go all out to rehabilitate them, or at least control them in less degrading conditions. (loc. cit., p. 232)

But if people were so efficiently 'controlled' that they became incapable of moral rulebreaking (a state of affairs which in any case I find inconceivable), their 'virtues' would vanish with their 'vices'. The elimination of punishment from social relationships would only be possible along with the elimination of the whole moral order of life.

Neither of these lines of criticism, then, seem to me to make much progress against the Hart account. There are, however, at least three other sorts of criticism which do seem to me, by contrast, to be on the right lines. One of these (e.g. Kemp, 1954) suggests that far more analysis needs to be made of the relationship between pain and evil. In the Hart account it is assumed virtually without question that pain is always evil and that therefore, since punishment is painful, it is an evil which could only be justified by showing it to be necessary to the avoidance of some *greater* evil than itself. Much wider issues than punishment, of course, are implied here. Without getting involved, however, in a full-scale discussion of hedonism (see for example Moore, 1903, chapter 3; Cowan, 1968), it is possible, I think, at least to suggest that there is room for doubt about the necessary evil of *all* pain. If I have toothache, for example, is my pain 'evil'? If I get kicked on the shins during a football match, is the pain of this an 'evil'? If, in making prodigious efforts to arrive at some crucial judgment or solve some intractable problem, I experience at times the 'pains' of frustration, anxiety, disappointment and so on, are these 'evil'? And if, in particular, a group of children, for example, cold-shoulder or rebuke a member of their group who is persistently spoiling what they are doing, or if between two friends a painful estrangement occurs because of some insensitivity or misunder-standing on the part of one or the other, or if a parent smacks a child because of some wilfully absurd, destructive or cruel piece of behaviour, *must* we say in any of these cases that the pain was necessarily 'evil'? Doesn't the judgment as to whether it was 'evil' or not occur as part of a moral judgment taking account, not just of the existence of the pain, but of the wider context of actions and relationships in which the pain occurred? Wouldn't we say, for example, that pain deliberately inflicted *for no good reason* was 'evil'? But to assume that the pain *of punishment* is inflicted 'for no good reason' is to beg the very question which the practice of punishment *raises*—namely, *is* there (in the particular case before me) 'good reason' for deliberately causing pain to the individual concerned?

There is therefore a real problem for the Hart account here, as it seems to me. I can understand how causing *pain* can sometimes be accounted 'good', but I cannot understand how one could ever do something 'good' by doing *evil*. Does any teacher who believes in punishing children for wrongdoing really think of himself as there-by doing something *evil* (rather than just painful)? If so, would it not be better for him to abandon the practice forthwith? But this, as I have already argued, is scarcely *possible* (without abandoning moral relationships with children altogether). Far better, then, that he should revise his *thinking* (his 'theory') about what he claims to be doing in practice.

The second line of criticism of the Hart theory which looks to me as though it could be fruitful is closely related to the first. Defenders of the theory have often argued that if punishment is interpreted from a retributive point of view solely, or in other words is construed as being in some sense a 'morally fitting' response to wrongdoing rather than merely a necessary evil, then it will follow logically that wrongdoers have a moral *right* to be punished—and, as Quinton puts it:

> It is an odd sort of right whose holders would strenuously resist its recognition. (Acton, op. cit., p. 57)

But is it in fact *true* that those who believe themselves to deserve punishment 'strenuously resist' it? Or, to put it another way, is it true that punishment inevitably *brings about* 'estrangement', to use Peters' words, and 'alienation' (loc. cit., p. 273 and p. 276)? I am not sure that this is just an empirical matter of what the facts are, as Peters says and as Quinton implies, or whether it is not a logical point also. On the matter of fact, however, in my experience punishment often *reduces* 'estrangement' and 'alienation' rather than causes it. Indeed it often seems to me that it may have been precisely *because* some estrangement has already occurred between, say, parent and child that the latter starts behaving in the way which later comes to merit punishment. The estrangement comes *before*, not after, the punishment. Punishment in a sense heals the breach—not by 'generating remorse' (which in any case is already there, if the child already feels that he *deserves* punishment) but by re-establishing the active personal relationship which estrangement seemed about to destroy. *Not* to be punished, when one feels that one deserves to be, is in fact (and I am not sure that logically the facts could be interpreted otherwise) to be treated either as being not worth bothering about, or as being beyond redemption anyway. Certainly, in my experience, children, far from 'strenuously resisting' the recognition of their right to be punished when they deserve it, usually seem determined to *ensure* that they will get it, by behaving in ways which grow steadily more demanding, less possible to overlook, the longer their punishment is delayed.

Quinton's phrase, 'an odd sort of right', deserves much more discussion than I can give it. Essentially, however, I think that Miller, for example, who is among those who have criticized it, is right when he says:

> ... just as statements or commands can only be addressed to those who understand them, or are capable of understanding them, so punishment can only be inflicted on those who are

> capable of appreciating its point ... the expression 'a right to punishment' is to be construed as meaning that the offender has the right to be regarded as a responsible person. (1966, p. 260)

Children who do *not* see the point of punishment certainly would not conceivably regard themselves as ever being entitled or as 'having a right' to it. If they received it nevertheless, it would indeed be odd if they did not 'strenuously resist' it and if they were not 'alienated' and 'estranged' from those who delivered it. On the other hand, to the extent that a child, at whatever age and stage, *is* beginning to see its moral point, rather than to interpret it merely as an attempt at psychological coercion, then being punished for wrongdoing will seem like having the existence of a moral order of things, and of one's place in it, confirmed. *Not* being punished, in such circumstances, could lead only to bewilderment, despair or indifference.

This brings me to the third example of the kind of criticism of the Hart view which I believe would be worth further thought. Many writers, utilitarian and retributivist alike (e.g. McCloskey, op. cit.; Goldinger, 1965; Kaufman, 1959; McPherson, op. cit.), have criticized Hart's basic strategy in trying to treat the point and the purpose of punishment as logically independent matters. To Hart, punishment's *point* is moral, its *purpose* social; or, to put it another way, its *meaning* is retributive, its *function* utilitarian. Critics of this strategy argue (rightly, I think) that one cannot logically disconnect function and meaning, or purpose and point, in this way. Once again, as in the earlier question about the 'evil' of pain, wider issues are involved than those of punishment alone. In educational terms the argument is similar to the question of whether 'methods' can be considered apart from 'content', in political terms to whether bad means can ever issue in good ends, in ethical terms to whether judgments about the 'rightness' of an action can be separated from judgments as to the 'good' which may come of it ... and so on. In terms of punishment, however, there is room at least for doubt, I think, whether social control, which in Hart's account is something whose point is *extrinsic* to the point of punishment, is the *purpose* of punishment at all. It may sometimes be a *consequence* of punishment, but this will depend on the morality of the society in which it is occurring. In an immoral society the consequences of moral behaviour (including punishment) are more likely to seem to members of that society to constitute *disorder*, than order. But in any case, whether or not the consequences of punishment (and of other forms of moral behaviour) contingently support the prevailing social order, consequences are not the *same* as purposes. In the Hart account the *point* of punishment is said to be a moral one. With this I agree, but *from* this it seems to me to follow that its purpose or function must be a moral one also.

6 Punishment and education

Rather than travel too far into the labyrinth of philosophical controversies about punishment, I have been concerned principally in this chapter to sketch one broad contrast. Punishment, I have suggested, is part of our education. It helps to initiate us, to use R. S. Peters' word, into the moral dimension of life. By contrast, but of course not necessarily in *opposition* to this, extrinsic controls which in psychological and legal contexts are usually misrepresented *as* punishments are described more clearly, I have argued, not as 'punishments' but as 'penalties'. Thus, for example, penalties can be awarded only by some agent formally authorized or empowered to do so, but one can be punished by *anyone*, I think, with whom one shares an interest. The rules governing the authorization of those empowered to impose penalties are quite separate and different from the rules which they are thereby made responsible for enforcing, but in the case of punishment the two sets of rules are identical—only a moral agent, in other words, is capable of punishing and of being punished. One is penalized for infringing the authorized rules of any social practice in which one engages, but one is punished for breaking specifically *moral* rules. A rulebreaker is liable for a penalty whether or not he can see good reason for the rules, but a wrongdoer is liable for punishment *because* he can see good reason for the rules (and has nevertheless broken them). Penalties are awarded 'disinterestedly'—the law is no respecter of persons—but punishments are as variable as the strength of interest of the persons concerned. One is penalized for failing to behave in a way which neither you nor your judge necessarily regard as being of any *intrinsic* importance (e.g. feeding a parking meter), but one is punished by someone with whom one claims to share an interest but towards whom one has failed to behave in a way appropriate to the interest which you share. A penalty is a disadvantage, in respect of the pursuit of personal goals. A punishment is more likely a timely reminder of what one's personal goals *are*.

These are some, at least, of the contrasts which seem to me implicit in the distinction which I have tried to draw between penalties and punishments. In educational situations it is the former, not the latter, which constitute any kind of 'last resort'. It is when children are *not* 'learning through interest' that we are inclined to fall back on extrinsic controls. When they *are* learning, they are learning about the *moral* value, as well as the other values, of their interest. Reward and punishment, then, must from the outset of such situations be an essential ingredient in what goes on. Of course it *hurts* to be shown that one has failed to do the very thing that one was ostensibly trying to do, but the fact that it is painful no more makes it wrong to be shown this, than the fact that a reward would be pleasant gives one the right to receive it. Educational situations are *intrinsically* rewarding, and therefore intrinsically *punishing* too. I don't see that they could be one if they were not also on occasion the other. And where people, such as teachers, claim to be *deliberate* agents in the education of others, then this must mean, I think, that on occasions what they *deliberately* do will hurt, just as on other occasions it will please. Exactly what it will take to 'show' a child for sure that he is failing educationally, is an empirical matter which will vary from child to child. It will depend partly, for example, on what sort of language he is thus far capable of understanding—words, gestures or deeds. But, whatever language is employed, it will have *force*, as well as meaning. It will perform a function, as well as 'say something'. Although this distinction between the force and the meaning of language was elaborated by Austin (1962) chiefly with the language of *words* in mind, rather than that of expressions, gestures, deeds and so on, it is no less applicable to the latter. With highly articulate children reward and punishment may often be accomplished by 'doing things with words'; with others—for example with very young children—it will be a matter, at least to begin with, of saying things with deeds. In either case, however, the *force* of what we say or do in punishing hurts, while the *meaning* educates. To a college student, for example, the force of a criticism can be painful, its meaning educative. To a very young child, the meaning of a smack can be educative, while its force hurts. But no general rules can replace the judgment which achieves value in each particular case. The art in education, whether undertaken by parent, teacher or anyone else, lies in understanding the language and in appreciating the sensitivity of the person whose interest one shares and therefore *in* whose interest one is concerned. With this understanding and appreciation one may begin to speak in a language which will be intelligible and with a force which will be sufficient for its purpose.

Where, however, the hurts which we inflict upon children and others are calculated by standards and imposed for purposes *extrinsic* to those of the situation in which they occur, we are dealing with penalties, not punishments, and not with discipline but with control. The contrast which I have tried to bring out in chapter 3 between discipline and control raises further questions about whether 'positive freedom' (through social control) is 'freedom' at all, rather than, say, paternalism or authoritarianism in disguise; and whether 'negative freedom' (which depends upon disciplined personal relationships) is possible at all, particularly for children, without the degeneration of social order into anarchy, aimlessness and arbitrary permissiveness. These issues may be pursued, for example, in J. S. Mill's *On Liberty* (edited by Warnock, 1962) or in the last two of Berlin's *Four Essays on Liberty* (1969). Meanwhile the compromise which I have suggested, in line with the compromise sketched in chapter 2, is that while *some* (the minimum) control is plainly necessary on grounds of prudence, our *educative* concern is with matters of discipline and not with matters of control at all.

Similarly, the contrast which I have presented in the current chapter between penal systems of control and the retributive (or punishing and rewarding) features of *any* more or less disciplined personal relationship raises questions, not only about punishment itself, but also about moral education and the ways in which, from their earliest days, children can begin to understand punishment as something more than just getting hurt or of being made to suffer a penalty when one does something which does not fit in with other people's settled ways of seeing things. The most interesting work in this field, after Piaget's, is that of Kohlberg (1966).

It is impossible, moreover, to consider questions about how children learn the force and meaning of words such as 'fairness', in abstraction from questions about social justice (Tawney, 1952) or the 'fairness' of the society *into which* those children are growing up. It is odd (to say the least) that while we seem often so ready to believe that children need to be *schooled* into adopting an adult 'moral' point of view, we ourselves, though adult and no doubt well-schooled, still seem to have the greatest difficulty in accepting and living by it. In the same way, it is unconvincing to say that children learn to be 'moral' largely by 'internalizing' *our* rules and standards, when whether or not our rules and standards *are* moral is still so very questionable. Might not schools sometimes be more *educative* places if we thought of them as providing opportunities occasionally for children to become *less*, not more, like us?

No doubt, therefore, I have raised many more questions than I have settled, but it has not really been my purpose in this book to settle questions, so much as to question that very *settled* institution of 'schooling' as a result of which, in my experience and to my way of thinking, so much *intrinsically* worthless time is spent both by children and by teachers in schools.

Conclusion

We may talk about 'education' in a descriptive or in an evaluative sense (see Peters, 1970). The descriptive sense is the one to which I have been referring throughout as 'schooling'.

Schooling is value-neutral. There is no intrinsic virtue in it. It is just what happens in a school—and 'schools' can be found anywhere at all where members of a group are coming into or towards conformity with a pre-existing norm which is relatively fixed, settled and inflexible. We talk of a school of whales or porpoises, a poker school, a drinking school, a school of thought and even, wonderfully, a school of education.

Schooling is what some sociologists describe, or used to describe, as 'socialization' (e.g. Elkin, 1960); or else they say that *education* is 'socialization', which is what goes on in schools. Thus, as a descriptive term employed in a supposedly value-neutral science such as sociology, 'education' is schooling. As such, its only value lies not in what it *is* to those engaged in it, but in what it is said to be *for* by the external observers who are doing the 'describing'. Just as the value of a penal system may be described as lying not in what is found to be *in* it by those undergoing it (e.g. its morality, or lack of it) but in what is actually seen by outsiders to come *out* of it (e.g. the upkeep of the rule of law, perhaps, through the deterrent effect of penalties), so the only value of a school system may be described as deriving not from what it is to those *in* it (e.g. a place of relative safety in which to develop an educated interest in life with other people) but from the value of some future or eventual life *outside* it. To those outside, it is seen and therefore described merely as a prerequisite to that eventual life.

By contrast, when we talk about 'education' in the evaluative sense, we mean something which to those engaged in it is valued intrinsically. Its only describable use or purpose, then, *is* to get people more educated. The only end to which education is the means is more education. The only 'needs' which education 'satisfies' are 'educational needs' ... and so on. To ask, then, whether 'education' is worthwhile, or what it is *for* or what justifies it, is not a request for information—and in *that* (informational) sense it is a non-question. It is like asking whether there is any value in engaging in something in which, already, one finds value. This is a request, not for information, but for an *explanation*.

Educational talk which purports to be explanatory but which says nothing more, in effect, than that education is worthwhile because it is worthwhile, is of course totally unconvincing. It involves what philosophers call a 'definitional stop' and is thus similar, as Hart points out (loc. cit., pp. 5-6), to the merely definitional 'justification' of punishment which retributivists employ when they say that punishment is justified because it is retributive —which is like saying that punishment is justified because it is just. It is because this answer sounds, and is, so unconvincing that Hart goes on to give a *utilitarian* 'justification' of *retributive* punishment, a justification not in terms of desert but of need. Instead of saying merely that the good reason for punishing people is that they deserve it, the utilitarian 'answer' is that some people *need* to be punished for other people's sakes. But this is an answer in terms of *information* purporting to tell us about *other* values to which punishment may be useful as a means, rather than an answer in terms of some *explanation* of the value of punishment in itself.

Similarly, when people start asking what education is for, the temptation is great to give a rousing answer in terms of information about some large, substantial, unquestionable sort of 'need' such as the transmission of our social heritage, or the preservation of what is best in our cultural tradition (including an ability to change it in a 'cultured' way), or, in more individual terms, our 'need' for all-round development, or socialization, or personal autonomy and rational choice and so on.

Certainly, to answer questions about what education is *for* in terms which sound merely like a definitional stop to further questions, by saying that education is intrinsically worthwhile, will not *convince* anybody. For example, it will not convince the politician who wants to know why teachers should have a pay rise, rather than, say, nurses or postmen or merchant seamen. It will not convince ratepayers who might rather see their money spent on the visible and exchangeable utilities of houses and shopping centres, than on the nebulous and seemingly useless 'values' of the local play-about primary school. It will not convince parents, either, if for example their children at the local secondary modern or creamed-off comprehensive seem unlikely, from those disadvantage-points, to have much of a chance of reaping the one substantial benefit which education *does* seem to be of some visible use for, namely, the acquisition of qualifications for a status career. (Anyway, say some parents, my boy can earn more as a lorry driver, so you can keep your status. I don't want his chances spoilt by your 'education'.) Finally, of course, an answer in terms of its intrinsic value will not convince children themselves, who want to know why they must or even *should* take a certain subject or do a certain task in school. If they were already *finding* it to be of value, they would not now be asking what it was valuable *for*. (They could, however, be asking for information which would help them in the *pursuit* of what they value, or for some explanation of things whose value they can *see* but not yet fully understand.)

The temptation, in all these cases, is to give an answer in terms of information about the possible *utility* of education for something which is itself not necessarily educative at all, but which one judges to be the sort of thing which will induce the questioner to put an extrinsic value on his education. Thus, to the politician for example, one points to the utility of education for raising national productivity, to the ratepayer one points out the utility of playing at shops as a preparation for the 'serious' business of counting your change in later life, and to the parents one explains that much of the secondary curriculum is in fact being geared nowadays to modern children's 'vocational needs'. To the child himself one gives a star, point, mark, grade or some other reward-substitute, adding that when he has got enough of these he can cash them for a qualification, which he can cash for a job, which will earn him further reward-substitutes, which he can cash for the 'necessities' of life (plus perhaps a few unnecessary but gratifying luxuries for his leisure time), so that he can go on working for a *better* job, earning *more* reward-substitutes, cashable for *more* necessities, *more* luxuries ... and so on. Does this sound like a travesty of the value of education? I certainly hope so—but it is quite a fair *explanation*, I think, of the value of schooling. To treat *education* as something of no intrinsic value but, at most, a way of laying up a useful store of knowledge, attitudes, and skills in order to sustain one's 'needs' until the great day dawns (e.g. on retirement) when at last one will be 'free' to do what one can see the *intrinsic* point and value of doing, is to turn 'education' into a sort of confidence-trick. Although it is unconvincing to say that education just *is* 'intrinsically valuable', to say that it is valuable *only* because it is needed for something extrinsic to it, is a travesty of the truth.

It is for this reason, then, that ultimately one has to explain what *is* intrinsically valuable in education, or in other words what 'intrinsically valuable' *means*. It is this which for example R. S. Peters is doing, I think, when he talks about the criteria of 'education' in the first two chapters of *Ethics and Education* (1966). And it is this which Dewey also was doing, when he talked about the criteria of 'educative' experience in *Experience and Education* (1938, chapter 3). But such talk is itself an attempt to *teach* us the meaning of 'education'. We can only learn from it if already we can to some extent *see* (though not fully understand) the point of the word. As an attempt at communication it is fundamentally no different from what a teacher is doing when he tries to help a child to 'learn through interest'. Unless *we* take education to be of value, there is no point in our reading Peters' or Dewey's account of it. Similarly, unless a child already finds *some* intrinsic point in his school curriculum, there will be no way in which his teacher can explain to him anything *more* of its value.

'Taking something to be of value' is what I have identified in this book with the notion of 'taking an interest'. 'Learning through interest', then, is *educative* learning. *Educative* teaching is trying to help someone to discover more of the point of what he finds interesting and thus is already inclined to pay some serious attention to. There is no end to the process. As one understands more, so there is more to understand. Subjectively, the value of one's interest grows, the more educated it becomes. Objectively, what one is interested *in* changes, as one's understanding of it changes. When interest is keen, then teaching is most straightforward. When pupils are puzzled, then the personal and intellectual discipline of both teacher and pupils is most on trial, because it is at this point that *both* may 'lose interest'. If, at this point, the teacher feels (as understandably he may) that he has to import extrinsic controls and considerations into the situation, then, for the time being, nothing educative is going on. We are left *just* with schooling.

What most needs explaining still, or next, in all this, is the *precise* nature of the two different relationships of means to ends involved on the one hand in education, on the other in schooling. We may express this for the time being as the difference between 'intrinsic' and 'extrinsic' values, but it would take another book to explore means-ends relationships thoroughly from this angle (see, for example, Taylor, 1961, chapters 1 and 12; Stevenson, 1944, chapter 8; or, for good, briefer articles, Beardsley, 1965, and Duncan-Jones, 1958). Alternatively we might tackle the distinction by trying to contrast pragmatism (or the view that activities are valuable when they are 'instrumental' or 'operational' in relation to their ends, *whatever* those ends are) with utilitarianism (or the view that value resides only in what is of 'utility' in relation to a single, general end such as 'the general interest'), but this, too, is well beyond the scope of my present inquiry (see, for example, Ayer, 1968). Again, we might tackle it by some frontal assault on the difference between doing something which is the 'means' of doing what we value (or, doing it *means* that we 'value' it) and doing something because it has been *evaluated* as being normally a 'good' sort of thing to do. This is the kind of comparison (between 'valuation' and 'evaluation') which R. B. Perry was especially concerned to make, for example, in his essay 'Value as any object of any interest' (reprinted in Sellars and Hospers, 1952). But both 'valuing' and 'interest' are notions far more complex, I think, than Perry made them appear (see, for example, Stevenson, 1963, chapter 2).

In the end (so far), it is the difference between what is 'interesting' and what is 'in someone's interest' which seems to me best to catch the flavour, as it were, of the difference between an educative and a non-educative situation, rather than the similar sorts of distinction which I have just enumerated, between 'intrinsic' and 'extrinsic' values, 'instruments' and 'utilities', what is 'valued' and what is 'valuable'. Fortunately, in school and in life the two may often coincide. In practice, we do not have to adopt an either-or attitude to them, or not all of the time. What is interesting to someone may be also, on occasion, in his interest. What we find intrinsic value in can also be of value for extrinsic ends.

When, for example, in valuing my garden, I mow the lawn (because this action is instrumental to that value, as I see it), mowing the lawn is 'normally' *also* of service or utility to me in other ways, such as giving me healthy exercise. What is interesting to me, therefore, in this case, is also what I would normally be said to 'need'. Nevertheless, to treat my lawn-mowing as though it were *only* something which I 'needed' to do, is to miss out or overlook what is *specifically* valuable in it, in favour of its very *general* serviceability or utility for all manner of other ends, such as getting exercise, or pleasing my wife who wanted the lawn cut, or my children who wanted a go at the lawn-mower. If I were just doing it, say, for the exercise, I could as well meet my need by turning the mower upside-down and trundling it up and down the path. Assuming, however, that I find some intrinsic point in mowing the lawn (because a mown lawn is part of what I *mean* by what to me is the 'good' of my garden), then to treat lawn-mowing merely as something of *general* utility will devalue it or trivialize it, putting it on a level of value the same as that of any *other* activity which would meet my needs equally well.

To take another example: one devalues or trivializes (by over-looking or missing the point or particular interest of) a spanner, say, as opposed to a pair of pliers, or a genoa jib as opposed to a spinnaker, or a minor as opposed to a diminished seventh, if one makes no distinctions between the hundred and one *equally* useful jobs which in each case *both* can do and for which, therefore, *both* can be said to be 'needed'. In the same way one devalues, say, food, if one *only* eats it because one 'needs' it. Just as children do not specifically *need* the education which they may get at school, so I do not specifically *need* the taste, say, of an orange: I just 'need' vitamins. To eat the orange only for its vitamins, or to value it only for its biological uses and not for its unique interest *as an orange*, is to treat it as something of no *particular* value and, ulti-mately, to devalue it altogether. 'Eating oranges' then becomes a mere token activity for 'getting vitamins', among innumerable other activities which might do the job equally well. The most useful token of this sort, of course, is money, which indeed is designed merely to be of value *as* a token (see Barry, 1965, p. 176). And just as eating *only* because one needed to could be thought of as part of the 'price' one has to pay for staying alive, so a 'needs-based education' might be part of the price which a child today might have to pay for 'getting schooled'. But mere 'staying alive' (plus getting a few luxuries now and then) is the same travesty of the possibilities of value inherent in life that mere 'getting schooled' is of those of education.

'Tokens' and 'types', which I have introduced in the above para-graph, form yet another pair of terms in which to try to speak of the distinction with which I have been concerned throughout (see, for example, Ayer, loc. cit., chapter 4). When education is treated as having only a token value to be cashed later for something quite *different* from education, what we are really teaching children is how to operate with two quite distinct sets of standards, their own and ours. By teaching them that their interests are only of value in so far as they are serviceable for some end which *we* declare valuable but whose intrinsic point is here and now unintelligible to *them*, we are not educating their interests; we are just making them show allegiance to a set of values which they do not understand. What these children learn at school, then, is a set of double standards. And even when (or if), eventually, they 'internalize' the extrinsic ones, this does not magically transmute them into *intrinsic* ones, like metal into gold. Schooling never *turns into* education—but that is no reason for saying that no education can and should go on in schools. This, as Roger Wilson said in the passage which I quoted at the outset, is up to the teachers who work there.

Bibliography

ACTON, H. B. (ed.), *The Philosophy of Punishment*, London: Macmillan, 1969.

ADAMS, J., *The Herbartian Psychology Applied to Education*, London: D. C. Heath, n.d.

ARONFREED, J., *Conduct and Conscience*, New York: Academic Press, 1969.

AUSTIN, J. L., *How To Do Things With Words*, Oxford: Clarendon Press, 1962.

AUSUBEL, D. P., *Educational Psychology: A Cognitive View*, New York: Holt, Rinehart & Winston, 1968.

AYER, A. J., *The Origins of Pragmatism*, London: Macmillan, 1968.

BAIER, K., *The Moral Point of View*, 1965 ed., New York: Random House, 1958.

BARRY, B., *Political Argument*, London: Routledge & Kegan Paul, 1965.

BEARDSLEY, M. C., 'Intrinsic value' in *Philosophy and Phenomenological Research*, vol. 26, 1965.

BEARDSMORE, R. W., *Moral Reasoning*, London: Routledge & Kegan Paul, 1969.

BENN, S. I., and PETERS, R. S., *Social Principles and the Democratic State*, London: Allen & Unwin, 1959.

BERLIN, I., *Four Essays on Liberty*, Oxford University Press, 1969.

BERNSTEIN, B., 'Open schools, open society?' in *New Society*, 14 September 1967.

BERNSTEIN, B., 'A critique of the concept of "compensatory education"' in Rubinstein and Stoneman (ed.), 1970.

BERNSTEIN, B., 'Education cannot compensate for society' in *New Society*, 26 February 1970.

BEST, E., 'The suppressed premiss in educational psychology', 1962, in Komisar and Macmillan (ed.), 1967.

BINDRA, D., and STEWART, J. (ed.), *Motivation*, Harmondsworth: Penguin Books, 1966.

BRAUNER, C. J., and BURNS, H. W., *Problems in Education and Philosophy*, Englewood Cliffs, N.J.: Prentice-Hall, 1965.

BRUNER, J. S., *et al.*, *A Study in Thinking*, New York: Wiley, 1956.

128

BRUNER, J. S., *The Process of Education*, Cambridge, Mass.: Harvard University Press, 1961.

BRUNER, J. S., *On Knowing*, Cambridge, Mass.: Harvard University Press, 1964.

BRUNER, J. S., et al., *Studies in Cognitive Growth*, New York: Wiley, 1966(a).

BRUNER, J. S., *Toward a Theory of Instruction*, Cambridge, Mass.: Harvard University Press, 1966(b).

CLARK, M., 'Discipline: a developmental approach' in Stenhouse (ed.), 1967.

COWAN, J. L., *Pleasure and Pain*, London: Macmillan, 1968.

CREMIN, L. A., *The Transformation of the School*, New York: Random House, 1964.

DEARDEN, R. F., '"Needs" in education' in *British Journal of Educational Studies*, vol. 14, November 1966.

DEARDEN, R. F., 'Instruction and learning by discovery' in Peters (ed.), 1967.

DEARDEN, R. F., 'The concept of play' in Peters (ed.), 1967.

DEARDEN, R. F., *The Philosophy of Primary Education*, London: Routledge & Kegan Paul, 1968.

DECECCO, J. P. (ed.), *The Psychology of Language, Thought, and Instruction*, New York: Holt, Rinehart & Winston, 1967.

DECECCO, J. P., *The Psychology of Learning and Instruction: Educational Psychology*, Englewood Cliffs, N.J.: Prentice-Hall, 1968.

DEWEY, J., *Interest and Effort in Education*, Boston: Houghton Mifflin, 1913.

DEWEY, J., *Democracy and Education*, 1966 ed., Toronto: Free Press, 1916.

DEWEY, J., *Experience and Education*, 1963 ed., New York: Collier-Macmillan, 1938.

DREEBEN, R., *On What Is Learned in School*, Reading, Mass.: Addison-Wesley, 1968.

DUNCAN-JONES, A., 'Intrinsic value: some comments on the work of G. E. Moore' in *Philosophy*, vol. 33, 1958.

ELKIN, F., *The Child and Society*, New York: Random House, 1960.

ENTWISTLE, H., *Child-centred Education*, London: Methuen, 1970.

EVANS, K. M., *Attitudes and Interests in Education*, London: Routledge & Kegan Paul, 1965.

EWING, A. C., 'Armstrong on the retributive theory' in *Mind*, vol. 70, 1963.

FEINBERG, J., 'The expressive function of punishment' in *The Monist*, pp. 397-423, 1965.

FESTINGER, L., *A Theory of Cognitive Dissonance*, Evanston, Ill.: Row, Peterson, 1957.

GARFORTH, F. W., 'Values in society and education' in *Education for Teaching*, no. 64, May 1964.

GELDART, W., *Elements of English Law*, 1966 ed. (ed. Yardley, D. C. M.), Oxford University Press, 1911.

GOFFMAN, E., *Asylums*, 1968 ed., Harmondsworth: Penguin Books, 1961.

GOLDINGER, M., 'Punishment, justice and the separation of issues' in *The Monist*, pp. 458-74, 1965.

GRIBBLE, J., *Introduction to Philosophy of Education*, Boston: Allyn & Bacon, 1969.

HARE, R. M., *The Language of Morals*, 1964 ed., Oxford University Press, 1952.

HARE, R. M., *Freedom and Reason*, 1965 ed., Oxford University Press, 1963.

HART, H. L. A., *Punishment and Responsibility*, Oxford University Press, 1968.

HAVIGHURST, R. J., *Developmental Tasks in Education*, New York: David McKay, 1953.

HENDERSON, G. P., ' "Ought" implies "can" ' in *Philosophy*, vol. 41, April 1966.

HENDERSON, G. P., 'Moral pragmatism' in *Philosophy*, vol. 44, January 1969.

HILGARD, E. R. (ed.), *Theories of Learning and Instruction*, Chicago: N.S.S.E., 1964.

HIRST, P. H., 'The logical and psychological aspects of teaching a subject', 1967, in Peters (ed.), 1967.

HIRST, P. H., 'The logic of the curriculum' in *Journal of Curriculum Studies*, vol. 1, May 1969.

HOFSTADTER, R., *Anti-Intellectualism in American Life*, New York: Cape, 1962.

HOLLINS, T. H. B. (ed.), *Aims in Education*, Manchester University Press, 1964.

HOLT, J., *How Children Fail*, 1969 ed., Harmondsworth: Penguin Books, 1964.

HUDSON, W. D. (ed.), *The Is/Ought Question*, London: Macmillan, 1969.

HUNT, J. MCV., *The Challenge of Incompetence and Poverty*, Illinois University Press (Illini Books), 1969.

KAUFMAN, A. S., 'Anthony Quinton on punishment' in *Analysis*, vol. 20, 1959.

KAUFMAN, A. S., 'The reform theory of punishment' in *Ethics*, vol. 71, 1960.

KEMP, J., 'Pain and evil' in *Philosophy*, vol. 29, 1954.

KOHLBERG, L., 'Moral education in schools: a developmental view' in *School Review* (University of Chicago), vol. 24, 1966.

KOMISAR, B. P., and MACMILLAN, C. B. J. (eds), *Psychological Concepts in Education*, Chicago: Rand McNally, 1967.

LANGFORD, G., *Philosophy and Education*, London: Macmillan, 1968.

LEIBER, J., 'In respect of liking' in *Analysis*, vol. 28, June 1968.

LOCKE, D., 'The many faces of punishment' in *Mind*, vol. 72, 1963.

MCCLELLAND, D. C., *Personality*, New York: William Sloane, 1951.

MCCLOSKEY, H. J., 'The complexity of the concepts of punishment' in *Philosophy*, vol. 37, 1962.

MACCOBY, E. E., NEWCOMB, T. M. and HARTLEY, E. L. (eds), Readings in *Social Psychology*, London: Methuen, 1959, 3rd ed.

MACINTYRE, A. C., 'Against Utilitarianism', in Hollins (ed.), 1964.

MACLAGAN, W. G., 'Punishment and retribution' in *Philosophy*, vol. 14, 1939.

MCMURRAY, C. A., *The Elements of General Method*, London: Macmillan, 1924.

MCPHERSON, T., 'Punishment: definition and justification' in *Analysis*, vol. 28, October 1967.

MANSER, A. R., 'It serves you right' in *Philosophy*, vol. 37, 1962.

MANSER, A. R., 'Games and family resemblances' in *Philosophy*, vol. 42, July 1967.

MASLOW, A. H., 'A theory of human motivation' in *Psychological Review*, vol. 50, 1943.

MASLOW, A. H., 'Some theoretical consequences of basic need gratification' in *Journal of Personality*, vol. 16, 1948.

MASLOW, A. H., *Motivation and Personality*, New York: Harper & Row, 1954.

MELDEN, A. I., *Free Action*, London: Routledge & Kegan Paul, 1961.

MILLER, W. A., 'Mr Quinton on "An odd sort of right"' in *Philosophy*, vol. 41, 1966.

MOORE, G. E., *Principia Ethica*, 1959 ed., Cambridge University Press, 1903.

PASHMAN, J., 'Raziel Abelson on "Because I want to"' in *Mind*, vol. 77, October 1968.

PETERS, R. S., *The Concept of Motivation*, London: Routledge & Kegan Paul, 1960, 2nd ed.

PETERS, R. S., ' "Mental health" as an educational aim', 1964, in Hollins (ed.), 1964.

PETERS, R. S., *Ethics and Education*, London: Allen & Unwin, 1966.

PETERS, R. S. (ed.), *The Concept of Education*, London: Routledge & Kegan Paul, 1967 (a).

PETERS, R. S., 'In defence of Bingo: a rejoinder' in *British Journal of Educational Studies*, vol. 15, June 1967 (b).

PETERS, R. S., 'Education and the educated man' in *Proceedings of the Philosophy of Education Society of Great Britain*, vol. 4, 1970.

PIAGET, J. (tr. M. Cook), *The Origin of Intelligence in the Child*, London: Routledge & Kegan Paul, 1953.

PIAGET, J. (tr. M. Cook), *The Child's Construction of Reality*, London: Routledge & Kegan Paul, 1955.

PLOWDEN COMMITTEE, *Children and Their Primary Schools*, London: H.M.S.O. (Plowden Report), 1967.

RACHELS, J., 'On liking' in *Analysis*, vol. 29, March 1969.

RALLS, A., 'The game of life' in *Philosophical Quarterly*, vol. 16, January 1966.

RALLS, A., 'Rational morality for empirical man' in *Philosophy*, vol. 44, July 1969.

RUBINSTEIN, D., and STONEMAN, C. (ed.), *Education for Democracy*, Harmondsworth: Penguin Books, 1970.

RYLE, G., *The Concept of Mind*, 1963 ed., Harmondsworth: Penguin Books, 1949.

SAMEK, R. A., 'Punishment: a postscript to two prolegomena' in *Philosophy*, vol. 41, 1966.

SCHEFFLER, I., *Conditions of Knowledge*, Illinois: Scott, Foresman, 1965.

SEARS, P. S., and HILGARD, E. R., 'The teacher's role in the motivation of the learner', 1964, in Hilgard (ed.), 1964.

SELLARS, W., and HOSPERS, J. (eds), *Readings in Ethical Theory*, New York: Appleton-Century, 1952.

SMART, J. J. C., 'Free-will, praise and blame' in *Mind*, vol. 70, 1961.

STENHOUSE, L. (ed.), *Discipline in Schools: A Symposium*, Oxford: Pergamon Press, 1967.

STENHOUSE, L., 'The Humanities Curriculum Project' in *Journal of Curriculum Studies*, vol. 1, November 1968.

STEVENSON, C. L., *Ethics and Language*, New Haven: Yale University Press, 1944.

STEVENSON, C. L., *Facts and Values*, New Haven: Yale University Press, 1963.

SWIFT, D. F., *The Sociology of Education*, London: Routledge & Kegan Paul, 1969.

TAWNEY, R. H., *Equality*, 1964 ed., London: Allen & Unwin, 1952.

TAYLOR, C., *The Explanation of Behaviour*, London: Routledge & Kegan Paul, 1963.

TAYLOR, P. H., 'The Plowden Report and the aims of education for the middle years' in *The Middle Years of Schooling*, Schools Council Working Paper No. 22, London: H.M.S.O., 1969.

TAYLOR, P. W., *Normative Discourse*, Englewood Cliffs, N.J.: Prentice-Hall, 1961.

TEEVAN, R. C., and BIRNEY, R. C. (eds), *Theories of Motivation*, Princeton, N.J.: Van Nostrand, 1964.

THALBERG, I., 'Remorse' in *Mind*, vol. 72, 1963.

THOMPSON, D. F., 'Retribution and the distribution of punishment' in *Philosophical Quarterly*, vol. 16, 1966.

THOMPSON, K., 'Not so simple' in *New Society*, 30 April 1970.

TOLMAN, E. C., 'A cognition motivation model', 1952, in Teevan and Birney (eds), 1964

TOULMIN, S., *The Place of Reason in Ethics*, Cambridge University Press, 1950.

WALLER, W., *The Sociology of Teaching*, 1965 ed., New York: Wiley, 1932.

WARNOCK, M. (ed.), 'John Stuart Mill: *Utilitarianism, On Liberty ...*', and other essays, London: Collins, 1962.

WHITE, A. R., *Attention*, Oxford: Blackwell, 1964.

WHITE, A. R., *The Philosophy of Mind*, New York: Random House, 1967.

WHITE, J. P., 'Learn as you will' in *New Society*, 4 December 1969.

WILSON, P. S., 'In defence of Bingo' in *British Journal of Educational Studies*, vol. 15, February 1967.

WILSON, P. S., 'Review of Dearden, R. F., *The Philosophy of Primary Education*' in *Education for Teaching*, no. 77, Autumn 1968.

WILSON, P. S., 'Child-centred education' in *Proceedings of the Philosophy of Education Society of Great Britain*, vol. 3, 1969.

WILSON, R., 'Review of Elvin, L., *Education and Contemporary Society*' in *Education for Teaching*, no. 68, November 1965.

WITTGENSTEIN, L., *Philosophical Investigations*, Oxford: Blackwell, 1953.

WITTGENSTEIN, L., *The Blue and Brown Books*, Oxford: Blackwell, 1958.

WOODWORTH, R. S., 'A behavior primacy theory of motivation', 1958, in Teevan and Birney (eds), 1964.

WOOTTON, B., *Social Science and Social Pathology*, London: Allen & Unwin, 1959.